Nick and I

With all good wishes

Ray S.

CW01431259

THE NEW DAWN

The Revelation Of The 21st Century

Ray Soweto

NEW DAWN PUBLISHING

www. newdawnpublishing.co.uk

First published in Great Britain by New Dawn Publishing in 2008

Ray Soweto is hereby identified as the author of this work in accordance with sections 77 and 78 of the Copyright, Designs and Patents Act 1988

ISBN 978-0-9560202-0-8

Printed in Great Britain by CPI Antony Rowe, Chippenham Wiltshire SN14 6LH

New Dawn Publishing   P O Box 163   Knaresborough North Yorkshire HG5 5AD

To Em, for her love and understanding

For seekers everywhere

THANKS

I am grateful to the Penguin Group UK for permission to include the quotation from *The Penguin Dictionary of Philosophy*, edited by Thomas Mautner (chapter 1) and to the editor of the *Pharmaceutical Journal* to use material from my articles first published there (chapter 24).

Special thanks go to Nick Sumner of Digital Media Infrastructure Ltd of Harrogate who saw the raw text into print with care and expertise and who transformed my sketches into a book cover, always with calm forbearance at my electronic shortcomings. I am indebted to CPI Antony Rowe for their dedication from the outset to ensuring that the final text was correct in every last detail, any imperfections in that direction being entirely mine.

My most heartfelt thanks go to the originators and publishers of *A Course In Miracles*, my guidance for the last 15 years, and grateful thanks go to Margaret Bunney, who introduced me to the Course.

I should like to thank those who were sources of inspiration during the writing of this book: His Holiness the Dalai Lama, who daily demonstrates that politics based on love is a practical proposition; Aung San Suu Kyi, incarcerated woman leader of the nonviolent movement for human rights in Burma, who endures continual persecution with courage and dignity; His Highness King Mohammed VI of Morocco, who is liberating his country's women. For keeping me up-to-date with world affairs, and my conscience activated, I owe thanks to the editors and staff of *New Internationalist* and *Amnesty Magazine*.

ABOUT THIS BOOK

While I was writing this book, friends asked what was it about, and I was stumped for an answer. To say that in the early hours of a morning in April 2007 I had been told to write a book called *The New Dawn*, and that I was then given five chapters by some unknown helper whom I christened the Lecturer, would have tested their credulity. At first it tested mine, but I have had fifteen months to get used to the idea, although I still cannot be sure how much of the book I am solely responsible for. I do know that after the first five chapters it was a struggle, yet whenever I was stuck I seemed to be given a thought or a subject that moved me on.

The only aspects of the book I am certain about are that I was told to write it, that it says something of significance for some people at the beginning of the 21st Century, and that its prediction of a new spiritual awakening, the New Dawn, will be fulfilled.

When I was given the subtitle *The Revelation Of The 21st Century*, I shied away. It sounded too pretentious a claim. Then I recalled that the theme of the book is love, the only revelation that matters in this or any century.

Ray Soweto

DANGER - MEN OBSESSING

Women are. Men must do. Most women are content with themselves as they are. Men go out into the world to prove themselves. The more ego-driven become our leaders and disasters follow.

These are biological differences. It is no use arguing that women would have become explorers, great scientists, artist geniuses and tyrants if they had been given the chance. That fact is that to explore, to make scientific discoveries, to create great works of art or to become a tyrant you need to dominate, to assert that you can't stay at home to mind the children or do the washing because you have to go off and discover Easter Island, isolate plutonium, saw a dead sheep in half and put it in formaldehyde, or to make ready the gas chambers. So far in our history, to do anything novel or bloody and atrocious, you have needed to be a man.

The short and mostly wrong explanation is that men can't help dominating because of their testosterone. Testosterone makes men restive, makes them fight and procreate, can be helpful to up-and-coming tyrants, but is a hindrance when it comes to buckling down to the daily grind of a thousand-long series of experiments on the DNA of the axolotl or to spending four years on one's back painting a chapel ceiling. Men are driven to make discoveries in laboratories or particle accelerators, to hitting the headlines with an arrangement of bricks they have laid on the floor of the Tate Modern, or to racing or flying faster than any male has raced or flown before, because they need to justify their existence. Women have babies. And even if they choose not to, they do not feel compelled to go to the extreme lengths that men do to prove their worth.

Men start off well enough. A five year old male has exterior genitalia that can readily progress from limp to erect, and can at that stage feel superior to a girl with, at that stage, an unassuming cleft. By puberty the ascendancy has been reversed. The girl knows, although in most societies she will have been advised not yet to proceed to produce proof, that she can have a child, that her purpose is clear. A boy in his early teens is not at all clear about his role. He can easily prove his sexual potency, but he is aware that he is not yet capable of selecting and providing for a partner, is aware that he has a long way to go before he can compete with grown males. If his father is a successful male who has made his way in the world, the adolescent may feel inferior and decide not to compete. If his father is lacking in confidence and weak or, as is increasingly the case in the 21st Century, absent, the son may feel less capable or worthy than his friends with competent fathers.

Young men have to find their unsure way in the world, aware that they have to win a partner against competition from other men, to gain a foothold in an increasingly competitive work market. And fatherhood to the budding man is an uncertain mystery. Even now there are primitive tribes whose male members are not aware of their part in fathering children. Shakespeare observed in *The Merchant of Venice* that it is a wise father who knows his own son, and it is equally true that it is a wise son who knows his own father. DNA testing resolves that uncertainty, but sometimes the results are surprising.

Fatherhood comes to a man nine months after the fathering, when the conceptual event is at best a vague memory and at worst an unidentifiable one among a blur of many possibilities. The consequence is that fatherhood in a man cannot be equated with motherhood in a woman. A man must find his purpose, justify his existence, fill the void left at the core of his being through not knowing what he is here for.

It seems on the surface a paradox that men are the perpetrators of the world's atrocities and at the same time the instigators of religions. Women, ensconced within the security of their role as partner-mother, do not need to question the purpose of life. Men, unsure of their significance, create belief systems to justify their existence.

Not only are men the ones who have created belief systems, they are exclusively the ones who debate the merits or drawbacks of the systems themselves. Men are the philosophers. Philosophical agonizing, presented by men as a serious search for truth, is simply a symptom of men's obsession with finding purpose and meaning to life. If the truth had been susceptible to being revealed by philosophical argument and debate, given the calibre of the minds involved, it would have been unmasked by now. Had there been one pronouncement out of the millions put forth by philosophers that helped with understanding life or making us measurably happier, it would have been blazoned forth and attracted innumerable supporters. It would have formed the basis of a new world-sweeping man-made religion.

Out of the almost infinite volume of philosophical pronouncements, many could be quoted to show their pointlessness. One, from the Penguin *Dictionary of Philosophy*, will do:
'This dilemma (whether future events are predetermined by past ones), set out in chapter 9 of Aristotle's *De interpretatione*, illustrates the general problem of contingent propositions about future events. His own response, as interpreted by Ockham and by present-day philosophers, was to accept the law of the excluded middle, i.e. the truth of every disjunction of the form *p or not p* (which does not seem to imply fatalism), but to reject the principle of bivalence, i.e. the principle that every statement *p* is true or false (which does seem to imply fatalism). The problem is relevant to questions of determinism, free will, foreknowledge, predestination etc. It also gave the impulse to Lukasiewicz's devising a three-valued logic.'

Men began inventing religions before they started philosophising. Sun worship was the obvious beginning, because the Sun provides so many benefits. It rises reliably every day and gives us light, and sets equally dependably, often providing spectacular colour effects for our benefit. And the Sun provides warmth and, by helping plants to grow, feeds us.

It is a characteristic of many men that they are never satisfied with anything for long. Which has given us progress, but also Playstations and nuclear weapons. So Sun worship, sensible because sunshine makes us feel good, was no sooner established than Moon worship was being tried out and, before long, according to archaeological evidence, children's bones found in quantity at various sites indicated that the next new religion involved human sacrifice. The Incas - the Inca men that is - took religion a step further and made human sacrifice the key element of worship, requiring the hearts of sacrificial victims to be torn out of their living bodies in front of a large and enthusiastic congregation, the enthusiasm presumably deriving from relief at having avoided being chosen as one of the victims.

The Aztecs borrowed a god of the spring, Xipe Totec, from the faraway Yopi tribe and also gave him the job of looking after goldsmiths. In spite of his snappy name and his connection with jewellery, Xipi Totec also got bloodthirsty and demanded that humans were sacrificed in his honour. At least that is what his priests said, but we have to bear in mind that they were men.

Perhaps Sun worship was abandoned because the Sun seemed to early man, even though he couldn't at that stage do any measuring, a long way away. And since men were inventing the gods and religions, they could come up with gods that were nearer to home. Some were so near that they inhabited the home and were called hearth gods and, in China, kitchen gods. The Romans' hearth god was Vesta, whose temple in Rome housed the sacred flame attended to by the six Vestal Virgins chosen by lot from twenty girls of good parentage. The Virgins had to serve for thirty years and if they let the flame go out or lost their virginity the punishment was death, some say by starvation, others that it was by being buried alive, a distinction that can have mattered little to the victims.

It was of course men that made the Vestal Virgins subject to the death penalty, just as it was men who demanded that hearts be torn out of living sacrificial victims. The point, presumably, was that the men who had thought up the religions wanted them to be taken seriously and there's nothing like the death penalty or heart extrication to emphasize the point. When considering man's inhumanity to man, it has to be borne in mind that the ones responsible, the high priests and the leaders, were often men with damaged egos who were spurred on to become leaders or high priests by their very defects.

Men, when inventing religions as in any other field, were nothing if not ingenious. Just as civilizations were much more complex than hunter-gatherer societies, so their religions became more elaborate. In Egypt, Osiris was greatly revered as the god of fertility until about 2400 BC when he took on the extra job of personifying the dead king. Egyptian kings by that time were regarded as divine and on death they somehow became Osiris who was also the god of the underworld. In an unexpectedly democratic turn of events, Osiris eventually became the personification of all dead Egyptians, which sounds like a full-time job but Osiris was nothing if not versatile and found time to invent brewing as well.

The Greeks had fertile imaginations but they did not invent religions so much as gods. The Greeks not only had a word for it, they had a god for it. The Greek version of the beginning of the universe was a remarkable precursor of the Big Bang theory, with matter flying everywhere, the resulting havoc being presided over by the god Chaos. As there was no Earth as yet and no life around, it is difficult to see how there could have been a witness to the events but nevertheless word was passed down that the personal features of Chaos could not be described because there was no light by which he could be seen. The darkness, being Greek, also had to have a god and this was Nyx, sometimes Nox, who was Chaos's wife and was dressed all in black, although if there was no light she may have just looked that way.

The Greeks liked variety and were always deposing old gods and inventing new ones, which suggests that some men in a room somewhere had the job of thinking up new gods and finding ways to get rid of the old ones, rather as one suspects that there are men in a room somewhere thinking up Christmas cracker jokes. Chaos and Nyx produced a son, Erebus, and he grew up quickly and dethroned Chaos. Feeling lonely on the throne, he married his own mother Nyx, and the god couple produced two beautiful children, Aether, Light, and Hemera, Day, who, with the sort of genes they had, naturally deposed their father and mother. With Aether's light, they were able to see that the universe was still unordered and, thinking that they needed some help before they tackled the mess, they had a child, Eros, and with his help they created Gaia, the Earth. Eros, seeing that the Earth was bare and featureless, fired some arrows into her (Gaia was female) and Gaia, instead of being annoyed, produced greenery, mountainry and animals, birds and fishes. Gaia liked what she saw so much that she created Uranus, Heaven, which is a good point to leave the Greeks and their gods because Uranus and Gaia deposed Aether and Hemera and then produced twelve gigantic children, the Titans, who, the god creators being a particularly deranged lot by now, went in for mayhem and skulduggery on a massive scale.

The Romans, more intent on practical matters, like inventing central heating and conquering the known world, were not so interested in creating gods and took over the Greek ones and often those of the countries they conquered. Roman males were not very discriminating when it came to adopting gods in the lands they overran. In Persia they came across Mithras and quickly adopted him as a new deity. Probably what appealed was that Mithras was a warrior god and this attribute no doubt overcame his other drawbacks, like his being born out of a rock. Despite Mithras's rocky beginnings he was provided with a knife which enabled him to kill the sacred bull from whose blood came all the animals and plants useful to man. Mithras was also credited with being the giver of sunlight and fertile rain (the other sort was not mentioned) and although the Romans had plenty of gods already, they could not resist Mithras and brought him back to Rome. Once the army got smitten with the new god, the Mithraic cult spread rapidly round the Roman empire and became so popular that for a time it looked as if Mithras worship was going to replace Christianity. It didn't, but the sun still shone and the rain still fell, which suggested that the powers of Mithras had been exaggerated.

The Romans were no fools. Militarily unrivalled, they conquered the parts of the known world that seemed to them to matter, established good roads, a legal system that was on the whole far in advance of anything tried before and, apart from incursions into new territories, largely kept the peace. To the Romans, apparently content with their empire and their gods, it was a shock when one of their most revered emperors converted to Christianity, a fringe religion of ascetic fanatics.

No one can be sure why Constantine adopted Christianity. He may or may not have seen a cross in the sky before the battle at the Milvian Bridge and ordered the Christian monogram, a P dissecting a saltire or diagonal cross, to be painted on the shields of his soldiers. What we do know is that the Romans won the battle and that

Constantine attributed the victory to his newfound Christian faith. From that point on Constantine ascribed all his successes to the new religion and soon he was proclaiming the official toleration of Christianity. He even went a stage further and ordered the restoration of Christians' personal and corporate property seized under the previous persecutions.

The difference between the Roman adoption of their previous gods and their embracing the Christian one is that previously the appropriation had been arbitrary and dependant on the discovery of a new god in a newly conquered territory, whereas the adoption of Christianity was due to the influence and example of practising Christians. Constantine was impressed by the application put into their work by the Christians, by their abstinence from the pleasures of the world and by their conscientiousness. The Christians were not just worshippers of a different God. They worked harder and were better citizens.

The spread of Christianity was certainly remarkable. Jesus had recruited twelve followers including four uneducated fishermen, a tax collector despised by the Jews because he was working for the Romans, and two Zealots, dissidents who fiercely opposed Rome and its polytheism (Judas, as a Zealot, was disillusioned with Jesus's acceptance of Roman rule and turned to betrayal). Jesus's message of the availability of God to all, illustrated by a score or more parables, the Sermon on the Mount, a few straightforward pronouncements and miraculous healings, was simple. It was also so effective that the world must have been ready for the message. It has been estimated that by the time of the crucifixion Jesus had made five hundred converts. It was certainly an insignificant number, yet his disciples were motivated enough to spread the message throughout most of the known world.

We do not know if any of the men who invented and looked after the affairs of the old gods, the Religion Men, were converted to Christianity or if some of the converts took it upon themselves to become leaders of the movement, but the results are evident enough. For the Religion Men, the simple message wasn't enough. It would not do for Christians to meet in one another's homes or a simple larger building, and the Religion Men decided that huge and elaborate edifices must be erected in which to worship.

Neither could Christians continue simply as brothers and sisters in the faith. They needed priests to guide them and to pardon their sins, and the priests needed to be guided by bishops - it got worse - and the bishops competed against one another to build bigger and better cathedrals, which were and still are marvellous to behold for those who are interested in architecture but had nothing to do with Jesus's message. Jesus came with God's message of love and forgiveness. The Religion Men created Christianity and that church whose male priests believe that the Bible forebids women to perform this role.

But the Religion Men did much worse than set up religious dogma and bureaucracy. They decided that the holy book of the Jews, the Old Testament, should become part and parcel of Christianity. From then on Christianity was saddled with the impossible burden of the seven day creation, the barbaric laws of Leviticus which specify the death penalty for, among other misdemeanours, cursing one's parents, working on the Sabbath, taking the Lord's name in vain, and adultery, especially if you were a woman.

The early Jewish prophets believed that the Jews were a chosen people. The outstanding contribution of the Jewish race to civilized society in the sciences and the arts suggests that many of them are. Jews comprise about 0.02% of the world's population and yet they have received 129 Nobel Prizes, many more than countries with massive populations. The Jewish Religion Men would no doubt like to attribute the achievements of their people to Old Testament teaching and studying of the Torah. The fact is that almost all the outstanding Jewish composers, musicians, writers and scientists, understandably, rejected their traditional religion.

In spite of the nonsensical nature of much of the Old Testament, in which God is frequently reported to be angry or jealous or sometimes both, there are swathes of fundamentalist Christians who are convinced that it is their solemn duty to believe every word of the Bible. With Christianity encumbered with the laws of Leviticus and the rest of the Old Testament clutter, and the Religion Men themselves, it is scarcely surprising that Christianity is in decline.

The Anglican Church is currently being so torn apart by the warring between its members who tolerate homosexuality and those who are bitterly opposed to it, that it is in danger of breaking up. The Religion Men, it goes without saying, are opposed to homosexuality, mostly because of some adverse reference to it in the Old Testament. The Religion Men, after all, erected the edifice they call the Christian Church, Leviticus, jealous God and all, because they had not learned to fill the void in their souls by discovering God, and they are not going to give up their precious dogma without a fight.

The Religion Men could take a look - if their closed minds would let them - at the lives of the North American plains Indians whose emphasis on male aggression and physical courage, accompanied by the initiation torture necessary necessarily endured by young men graduating into the ranks of the braves, led to more sensitive males becoming squaw-men, dressing as women and opting out of the warring cycle of incessant tribal attack and retaliation. With the world men have created, it is hardly surprising that some men choose to take a more compassionate way or that some women prefer their own sex as partners rather than settling for men.

Men have not only created violence and atrocities in the world but, as Religion Men, they have taken Jesus's gospel of good news and turned it into a religion concerned with buildings, hierarchies of officials in different coloured robes and hats, a religion alarmed at the imagined affront of women priests and the fearful danger to the institution of expressing happiness in church. We in this country should not be surprised that the only section of Christianity with swelling congregations are the Pentecostal churches, many of them with a largely black membership, who experience the joy of God and feel the urge to express it.

The religion of Christianity, the one made by the Religion Men, reached its zenith during Victorian times, with church-going on Sundays *de rigueur* among the middle classes and, by a little arm-twisting, among their servants. Then, to his eternal credit, Darwin deduced how evolution worked, published his book *On the Origin of Species* in 1859, which demolished the Old Testament seven day creation myth and, thankfully, much of the religious edifice that went with it. In the meantime, while the established church was at last facing the fact that its Old Testament accretions had nothing to do with Jesus's message, John Wesley, his brother Charles, and the new Methodists were taking the original message to the section of the population the church had ignored, the industrial workers. The Methodists too put up buildings, but more modest ones, and built Sunday Schools, many of which provided schooling during the week. Although Christianity, the religion, is largely out of touch with Jesus's message, individuals within it, as the Wesley brothers showed, can and do arise and promote the original good news.

Christianity is not of course the only religion to suffer from the machinations of the Religion Men. Islam was rent by partisan Religion Men immediately after the death of Muhammad. The Sunnis, the 'traditionalists,' believing the Prophet had left no successor (*khalifah*, hence caliph), left the choice to two of Muhammad's fathers in law, highly respected early converts and trusted lieutenants, who selected Abu Bakr, father of the Prophet's favoured wife, A'isha. A separate faction believed that the Prophet had designated his cousin and son-in-law Ali ibn Abi Talib Shia, as his successor and these followers, the Shia, or 'partisans' of Ali, at first accepted a compromise, agreeing to Abu Bakr's leadership in view of Ali's youth. Abu Bakr, before his death, appointed 'Umar, as his successor, avoiding a caliphal election, but also ensuring the opposition of Ali's supporters, the Shia, in a classic Us and Them rift that has repercussions to this day.

The Religion Men in Islam and Christianity were and are agreed about one thing. Women must be kept in their place. It was an affront to male Christian priests to suggest that women might also be good at the job. It is the Religion Men of Islam who maintain social segregation of the women and who arbitrarily lay down dress codes not found in the Qu'ran. These same oppressors, fearful at women getting a taste of freedom, have decided that women must be shrouded from head to toe in black, the colour that is the least comfortable in hot countries because it absorbs more heat than any other. In Saudi Arabia, women may not drive a motor car.

The sadness about the great religions is that instead of their later leaders being ahead of their followers in terms of tolerance and enlightenment, they are always way behind. The archbishops and popes, the ayatollahs and the mullahs, usually do eventually see the light, but at the cost of their credibility, since they follow what the lay individual and the non-religious concluded long before. The Catholic church has relatively recently conceded that Copernicus's and Galileo's conclusions were right and that believing in heliocentricity is no longer a sin. Sometime in the future, Catholic leaders will cease preaching that it is against God's will that women with large families in poverty-stricken Africa and South America should practise birth control. The mullahs in Saudi Arabia will no doubt one day accept that it does not displease God a great deal if a woman drives a motor car.

Any catching up the religions do is likely to be futile, too little and too late, since the days of the dogmatic religions are numbered. Jonathan Swift summed it up when he remarked that we have just enough religion to make us hate, but not enough to make us love one another. Religions, however well meaning and inspirational at the beginning, end up as a catalogue of man-made beliefs which must be adhered to. Love cannot come from dogma, only from the heart.

Affluence and education have hastened the demise of the man-made religions. Sooner or later consumerism, the current obsession with the baubles of materialism, will pall. We have not faced up to it yet, but the current materialism, like practically all that is wrong in the world, stems from the same source. Our acceptance of male dominance.

2

THE   TROUBLE   WITH   MEN

The world is sick. In any illness there is a crisis, when the body overcomes the malady or succumbs to it. The world is at a crisis point now, and to heal we need a diagnosis. To diagnose, we need to look at the symptoms and to take a case history. The following symptoms are evident to anyone, although readers might like to add some of their own:

> War
> Genocide
> Dictatorship and tyranny
> Drug trafficking and addiction
> Political corruption

The case history reveals past symptoms of equally horrific atrocities that include the Holocaust, the Inquisition, gulags, apartheid and many more. Some of the symptoms, the Inquisition, the Holocaust and apartheid, are no longer in evidence although the memory of them is still disturbing to many. Slavery is officially abolished, but we know that many people are still condemned to live as slaves.

History tells us that the world has always been sick, and the Christian church, whose original message was hope, came round to the view that man is inherently sinful, just the opposite of what the founder preached. Despondency will not help. We have to face up to the fact that the world's sickness is more critical than ever before. But a crisis point, even one as grave as this, is a time of opportunity. To paraphrase Doctor Johnson, there is nothing like the prospect of imminent execution to concentrate the mind.

The diagnosis of the world's sickness presents us with a major surprise. If we look at the symptoms, the atrocities listed above and any others we like to add, it is evident that they are all perpetrated by men. It is not just that almost all of man's inhumanity to man is wreaked by males, it is inflicted by a tiny proportion of them.

The revelation that a small proportion of one half of the human race has been able to inflict so much misery on the rest should astonish us, rock us to our very foundations. It is our failure to acknowledge this obvious and glaring reality that has stood in the way of creating a better world. We are no longer outraged, not even surprised, by male tyranny and slaughter, let alone corruption and mismanagement.

Men have held a monopoly on the perpetration of atrocities because they have been in a position to inflict them. They have been the rulers. They have had the power. In the ape societies from which man evolved, alpha males rule, and the tradition was inherited by *Homo erectus* and then by *Homo sapiens*. Male leadership during man's hunter-gatherer era was an advantage since groups had a better chance of survival under a physically strong and courageous leader. Assertive ape-like leadership may have been necessary when hunter-gatherer groups were seeing off the sabre-toothed tiger or fancying mammoth steak for supper, but it would be incredible if we went on believing these to be the right credentials for leadership in today's technological democracies.

The whole of history is a testament to the atrocious potential of men, and in the last hundred years we have experienced horrifying reminders of the capacity of male leaders to turn psychopathic. The aspiring watercolourist became, as a leader, Adolf Hitler; the mild seminary novice, Josef Dzhugashvili, was transformed into Joseph Stalin; the idealistic student of human rights turned into Mao Tse-tung.

Even very recent history shows us to be unbelievably uncritical of male leaders. The American president and the then British prime minister, both supposedly Christian and God-fearing men, sent their countries' troops into Iraq, have been responsible for bombing and killing innocent civilians in order to remove a dictator, and in the process have presided over a country's bloody slide into civil war. And there has been scarcely any public outcry, hardly a voice raised in protest. Male leaders have always taken their countries into wars. What's new?

What will be new, is that the world is about to question the inevitability of accepting misrule by men. The next step is for the silent fifty per cent in democracies, the women, to wake up to their power potential, and for the great majority of men to realize that we are poised to share a better future. It is time for men and women to realize that wise and responsible leadership is not achieved by electing male leaders with charisma and inflated egos.

The notion has scarcely been aired, the seed only now planted and about to germinate, the idea ready to flower, that we in democracies have no need to tolerate men's misgovernment any longer. The progress of mankind has been, although with halts along the way and recent diversions into the dark alleys of communism and national socialism, towards freedom of expression, towards betterment. We no longer have to accept male leaders who assume that we will follow them however senselessly and misguidedly they behave.

Of course most men are caring partners and, on the whole, good fathers, although few are as good at being partners or parents as women are. Women have been so good at partnering and parenting that men have been allowed to get on with their business of going out to work or war, bringing in the money or the loot, running businesses and countries and generally having things their own way. Recently men have conceded that their partners can go out to work too if they feel inclined, as long as they're around to get the meals and to see to the children. Women, although many have not yet come to appreciate their own worth, can't help being good to children and men.

The male leaders' argument is that goodness is all very well in its place, but when it comes to running the world, goodness is not what is required. Hard decisions have to be made, decisions when goodness would be a hindrance, would be interpreted - by the other men decision makers - as weakness. The place for women and their goodness is at home where they won't get in the way of hard decision making. So it has been. And we have a world where in some countries individuals are eating themselves into obesity and an early grave, although not before straining their nation's health provisions to the limit, while in others, male war lords, either power crazed or religious fanatics, ensure that fighting replaces farming and that hundreds of thousands die from famine. Where indeed is the place for goodness in the world that men have made?

It was thought until recently that man was the only species on the planet that killed its own kind. Many male animals fight, especially in competition for female partners, but not usually to the death. We now know, through the observations of Jane Goodall and others, that chimpanzee males in groups of six or more regularly form raiding parties which, if they find a lone male of another group, will attack and kill it. We also know, from the work of Sibley and Ahlquist on ape and human DNA, that the human genome is closer to that of the chimpanzee than that of the gorilla, which is no great surprise since chimpanzees are nearer to human size and use more tools than gorillas do. What was not expected was the finding that chimpanzees are closer to humans than they are to gorillas.

Chimpanzee males exhibit another activity common to human males. Chimpanzee females, when receptive, are not too choosy and accept the advances of all males of her group except her maternal brothers. Normally the brothers accept rejection by their sisters, but occasionally a brother chimpanzee will go berserk at being denied, chase the sister, beat her into submission and rape her.

Men, like chimpanzees, form raiding parties bent on killing other males, and throughout history have frequently done it on a larger scale, with one army fighting another in pitched battle. If there is a series of battles we call it a war. Is then the urge for male football supporters to arrange pitched battles with those of an opposing team simply the expression of a genetic propensity, like that inherent in male chimpanzees? Is going to war a similar genetic response on a larger scale? The answer is that it does not matter. Most of us live in democracies or under systems that are closer to democracy than they have been in the past. We have no need to elect male leaders who will take us into wars, other than in the defence of their own country.

Neither does it matter if there is a genetic element to rape. Genetics may or may not make rape understandable. Either way it is intolerable. Rape cases needs prosecuting as rigorously as other forms of physical violence, and as often.

Political corruption, listed above as an atrocity, may not appear to be in the same league as war and genocide but, as we in the Western democracies are finding out, it strikes at the root of society. The awareness that one's rulers are not straight engenders feelings of helplessness and hopelessness in the electorate, and can contribute to the unease which increasingly finds expression in the resorting to alcohol or drugs. No one knows to what extent consumerism is fuelled by frustration at the deficiencies of politicians. But we can take heart. Political corruption is a male prerogative and the male monopoly of power is about to come to an end. Women are going to take up their long disregarded rights.

Although we do not need to go too deeply into the reasons for the male propensity for violence, torture and murder, since it is sufficient to condemn and as far as possible prevent it, there is a more subtle facet of male behaviour that needs understanding, what might be called men's progressive tendency. When Jacob Bronowski, in the early 1970's, presented his celebrated and seminal television programme on the rise of mankind from primitive origins to its contemporary elevated status, he called it *The Ascent of Man*, although The Ascent of Men would have been a more appropriate title. Seven women were given a mention in the series and in the resulting book: Queen Anne, because she knighted Newton; Queen Isabella I, because she, along with her husband Ferdinand, backed Columbus; Marie Antoinette, because she was, well, Marie Antoinette; Queen Victoria, because in her time she ruled the world's greatest power, and Madame Curie for obvious reasons.

One of the two other women who got a mention, Ellen Sharples, was included for the not so obvious reason that she made a pastel portrait of Joseph Priestley (an inclusion made even less worthy since Priestley discovered oxygen two years after the Swedish apothecary, Carl Wilhelm Scheele). One woman did get in on merit. Dame Kathleen Kenyon was from 1961 to 1966 director of the School of Archaeology in Jerusalem and was responsible for the excavation of Jericho to its Stone Age beginnings and for revealing it to be the oldest known site that has seen continuous occupation.

What the world remembers Jericho for is the siege that was won by Joshua, who organized a trumpet blast that collapsed the town walls, although that version is only for those who have not read the Old Testament. In the story told in Joshua chapter 6, Joshua got his priests to go round the city blowing their rams' horns once a day for six days while the rest of the Israelites kept quiet. On the seventh day when the priests started their trumpeting he ordered the Israelites to shout at the top of their voices and it was the shouting that collapsed the walls. Research, that spoilsport of all good stories, has shown that Jericho's clay walls were insubstantial and that when the townsfolk went up on the walls to see what all the shouting was about, the walls couldn't take the weight and collapsed. What followed was on Joshua's orders and, as the authorised version quaintly puts it, 'And they (the Israelites) utterly destroyed all that was in the city, both man and woman, young and old, and ox, and sheep, and ass, with the edge of the sword.' Joshua may have been a holy leader and a prophet, but he was also a man.

Bronowski could include such a mixed bag of token women in his account because it was so blindingly obvious that mankind had ascended almost entirely due to the efforts of men. But ascended to what? A world unthinkingly consuming the planet's resources at a rate that will bring impoverishment and chaos within the foreseeable future. With the citizens of the leading nation, the United States of America, devouring the Earth's raw materials at a rate that, if copied by the rest of the world's six billion population, would require the availability of six Earth-size planets.

America has, by comparison with India and China, a small population. The American mass-consumption way of life understandably looks attractive to the people of those countries where they are working for the equivalent of a dollar or two a month. If the population of China alone were to adopt the American rate of consumption, the planet would rapidly be bankrupt of resources, not to mention suffocating with pollution, and the great myth of the ascent of man would be replaced by the reality of imminent scarcity and decline. We need constantly to remind ourselves that the wrongs of the world are only there because of the policies pursued by the minority of men who run things.

In looking at the current state of the world there is no point in taking the apocalyptic view. Man has a great capacity to adapt and survive. But it *is* necessary to acknowledge the fact that it is men and male policies that are responsible for the catastrophes staring mankind in the face: failing resources, climate change and the globalisation of greed.

This is not the first time that the world has been in a mess. In fact one of the barriers to improving things is that history tells us we have always been in a mess. As far back as the 5th Century BC, Thucydides, a good historian though not a great thinker, was gloomily prognosticating in *The Peloponnesian War* that it is in the very nature of humans to act in the future as they have in the past. Thucydides could be forgiven for taking such a gloomy view. Athens had been defeated militarily and its moral decline was all too apparent after the glory years under Pericles. Plato too was concerned at the state of the state and blamed Athens' decline on the misrule of its democratically elected leaders, but instead of realizing that it was because they were *men* that they'd made a hash of things, he blamed democracy and the leaders' acquisitiveness. Rulers who got elected to power - and of course he was talking about men - got avaricious and exploited their citizens. The famous solution, in his *Republic*, was the creation of a class of Golden Ones who would rule, supported by the Silver Ones, the military, who would keep the Golden Ones in power and ensure that the Bronze Ones, the workers, toed the line. More or less what Hitler managed to get away with for a decade, and what Mugabe is inflicting on Zimbabwe today.

Since Plato, mankind has had time to look at quite a few alternatives to democracy and after the experiments with fascism, national socialism and, more recently, the collapse of communism (except for the variants practised in China, Cuba and North Korea), we've come to the conclusion that democracy works best. The collapse of communism, while hailed in the West as a huge endorsement of democracy and capitalism, was to some extent a Pyrrhic victory. Because the Soviet system was so politically repressive and economically unsound, its exposure and downfall has made us smugly complacent about democracy in its present form. We believe that as political systems go it is the nearest to perfection we'll ever get. Without male tyrants at the helm it might be. With that other male variant, messianic Christians, in charge, we end up introducing Iraq to the horrors of civil war.

Democracy, as Sir Winston Churchill so famously proclaimed, is the worst form of government except for all those other forms of government that have been tried from time to time. Democracy is our good and best hope, but only providing we put in place measures that prevent an elected leader taking actions against the will of the people, debar a leader from taking his nation, apart from in its defence, into war. Plebiscites and referenda are unpopular with political parties because they - we are talking about men - want to exercise their power without restraint, but democracy cannot work towards a better world without checks on male leadership. Politicians need to be reminded that the country's armed forces are under the control of a Ministry of Defence under the control of parliament and should not be available to a prime minister for senseless assaults on the inhabitants of countries whose leaders he and the American president happen to object to.

The failure of communism has had another adverse effect on the Western democracies, fostering the myth that unfettered capitalism brings the greatest good to the greatest number. The worshipping of strange idols has always been a male prerogative, as we shall see later, but since economics seems a far cry from Baal and Osiris, men imagine that idolatory of the free market is free from the dire consequences of the older transgressions. But any obsession leads eventually to disaster and the free market and monetarism are no exceptions.

The free market worked well to begin with, when a farmer with surplus corn exchanged a bushel or two for a goat or a bolt of cloth. The theory of the free market as now practised is that it makes a lot of money for those at the top of the pyramid, a contention not disputed, and lavish spending on goods and services by the wealthy helps those lower down by keeping them in work and boosting their earnings, the so-called trickle-down effect. The only snag is that it hasn't worked. Since 1951 the world's total economic output has increased more than five-fold, while the number of those living in absolute poverty has more than doubled. An equally calamitous outcome is that this scale of economic growth has pushed consumption of the planet's resources to unsustainable levels.

The advocates of the unfettered market, that is to say those who are benefiting from it most in material terms, go on preaching the gospel of economic growth when it is obvious to the most untrained observer that this is a recipe for disaster. The economic supremos in nearly every country on the planet are aiming for an annual economic growth of anything from one or two per cent to rises well into double figures, ignoring the fact that the world demand for resources is already unsustainable. The level of material wealth paraded by America and Europe, and which the rest of the world is desperately striving to emulate, is at the heart of the problem. There is no possibility that the world could sustain the planet's whole population at anywhere the levels enjoyed by the affluent West.

Decadence is usually a sign of the end of an era and we may take encouragement from the latest outbreak among city professionals in London of a decadent ritual first adopted in the fleshpots of St Tropez and Monaco. The participants are those made uneasy by their performance-related annual bonus expressed in six or seven figures, earned, if that is the term, by switching billions of dollars around the world's exchange mechanisms from low interest currency to higher interest currencies. To assuage their unease, all that is required is the hire of a large room at an exclusive club and a supply of the most expensive champagnes, preferably vintage Cristal at £280 a bottle or Dom Perignon at the give-away price of £165. The super-rich participants then spray the champagne over each other while drinking Belvedere vodka at £180 a bottle. At a typical such session not long ago in London W1 the champagne bill came to almost £22,000, the actual drinks a mere £4700. The bill for cleaning up the room was £15,000.

Any ritual that derides the concept of respect for ultra-expensive drinks is heartening, and is based on well established male traditions. Peoples in simpler and less wealthy cultures than our own, whom we in the contemporary urbanized world call primitives, on the death of a tribal chief - male that is - commonly call for a party attended by the males of neighbouring tribes and lasting for several days until the food and drink run out, a procedure that beggars the hosts for months or years afterwards. In the potlatching ceremonies hosted by the chiefs of North American Indians of the northwest Pacific coast, the feasting lasted several days during which the host chief indulged in ritual boasting and encouraged his guests to join him in the destruction of his most valued possessions, convincingly demonstrating to his guests the host's overwhelmingly superior wealth. Potlatching parties were made illegal in both the United States and Canada in 1884.

Champagne spraying and potlatching are typical male ego responses. To males in thrall to the ego, neither being a tribal chief or a top bonus earner in the city will satisfy, because the ego can never be satisfied. It will be more productive if we understand the male psyche rather than condemn its manifestations. We can look first of all at the worst cases and see why a tiny proportion of them become tyrants who murder by the million.

3

NASTY, BRUTISH AND MALE

Most men live law-abiding lives, do not indulge in violence against other men or their partners, work to provide for their families and behave decently. Yet a very few men have the determination and ruthlessness to become tyrants and to indulge their savage propensities.

We have three glaring examples in our recent history, in Stalin, Hitler and Mao Tsetung. In many countries psychopaths are put into prison, and in the more civilised ones into secure psychiatric care, yet tyrants are only fleetingly confined if at all. They seem from the outset to be larger than the system, to create their own rules, to be predestined to achieve power. And once in authority, to flaunt all the laws of decency, to defy all moral codes.

To understand tyranny we need to take a look at the tyrants. We can do no better than study the recent trio, the Tyrant Three, since they are relatively fresh in our minds and their lives well researched. Hitler, Stalin and Mao led very different lives, but they all had one thing in common, a difficult start in life.

Joseph Stalin as a boy was described in his national identity papers as Josif Djugashvili, peasant, from the Gori District of Tiflis Province. Both his parents had been born as serfs and had only been emancipated in 1864, fifteen years before Joseph's birth. On emancipation, Joseph's father became a cobbler in the small town of Gori, but it was no success story and he was a bitter man, a drinker, and regularly beat his wife and son. Joseph's closest friend at school later concluded, no doubt with the benefit of hindsight, that the severe beatings made Joseph as hard and heartless as his father, making him view all those in authority as hateful. Joseph was from the beginning, the friend said, determined to gain revenge against all in authority.

Hitler's start in life in rural Austria, in spite of the impression he gave in *Mein Kampf*, was more comfortable, his father having broken with the family tradition of employment as small farmers or village craftsmen and become an officer in the Hapsburg Imperial Customs Service. Alois Hitler did not beat Adolf but was authoritarian and aloof and showed no affection to his wife and son. The worst treatment Alois meted out to his son was to insist that he join the civil service, a fate Adolf was determined to avoid. Not that he had any concrete plans for his future. Adolf showed little interest in any subject at school other than art and spent his time playing war games and reading translations of Karl May's adventure stories about North American Indians. It seems more than likely that Hitler, an Austrian outsider isolated from the country he was to rule, identified with the American Indians who were forced into the role of outsiders in their own country. Stalin too was born on the fringes, in a Georgia annexed by Russia and reduced to a poverty-stricken province.

As is so often the case when a father is remote from his wife and children, the wife compensates for the lack of affection in her partner by forging close ties with her children. Joseph Stalin's mother, Ekaterina, doted on her son, and when her husband moved to Tiflis to take a job in a shoe factory, she went as housekeeper to an Orthodox priest and with the priest's help, enrolled Joseph in a church school. Ekaterina, determined that Joseph should become a priest, sacrificed her own comfort by finding the fees necessary to keep Joseph in the fee-paying church school. Joseph, as a boy, was no rebel. His singing voice attracted attention and he was happy to join the church choir. He worked conscientiously at his school subjects and won a scholarship to the Orthodox theological college at Tiflis. Throughout their childhoods and into their teens, both Hitler and Stalin were doted on by their mothers, an influence which when coupled with estrangement from the father, can lead not only to delusions of grandeur, but to an even worse outcome, to achieving positions of grandeur. Both failed to adjust to the communities they were born into, lacked normal emotional feelings and developed a belief that they were special, chosen by fate to achieve great things.

Mao had a more promising start to life than either Stalin or Hitler. He was born in the Shaoshan valley in Hunan, in the centre of China but not in touch with it, the valley of Shaoshan being still isolated, with neither roads nor navigable rivers. Even such an important event as the death of the emperor in 1908 had not reached Shaoshan two years later when Mao left the valley and heard the news.

Mao's father Yichang was better off than most of his neighbours in the valley, having married a local girl and then gone off into the army to earn enough to pay the family debts. Yichang could read and write, and as a soldier in the outside world he had picked up some business ideas. When he came back to his village, Yichang bred pigs and traded in top quality rice for selling at a nearby market.

Mao was not only better off than his friends, but he had been given propitious names. In China the first name, equivalent to a Western surname, may or may not have a special meaning but the other two names, usually now combined in English, are chosen with great care. The middle name, the clan name, Mao's *Tse*, was taken by all the children of that generation and Tse meant 'to shine on.' The third name, the second part of the combined two syllables, is specific to each child and the *tung* in Mao's case means 'the East.' Tsetung therefore meant 'to shine on the East.'

The Chinese traditionally are superstitious and although children are usually given a flattering or grandiose name, it is considered to be tempting fate if this is not modified by a more down-to-earth pet name. Mao was taken by his mother to an eight foot high rock thought to be enchanted and, after paying his respects to the rock with kowtows, he was considered adopted by the rock and took the pet name *Shi san ya-zi*, the Boy of Stone. This name appealed to Mao and he used it into adulthood, preferring it to his formal name, and one is left wondering if he had a premonition that his attitude to his people would be stony-hearted rather than illuminating.

Since Mao's mother was of the Wen family, and even after marriage she lived with them, rather than with her husband in Shaosan. Mao saw little of his father in his early years and, as with Stalin and Hitler, was doted on by his mother. She was gentle and easygoing, and later in life Mao would freely confess that he worshipped her, an emotional attachment he was never to show again. 'Wherever my mother went, I would follow ………. Going to temple fairs, burning incense and paper money, doing obeisance to Buddha…….. Because my mother believed in Buddha, so did I.'

Mao had an idyllic childhood until he was eight when, in the spring of 1902, he went to Shaosan under his father's care. Yichang was well off but remained a workaholic all his life and expected Mao to be equally diligent. Mao went to live with a tutor to study the Confucian classics, which was the only way of advancement in China at the beginning of the 20th Century. Mao had a good memory and did well at learning by heart the difficult texts, but found the routines irksome, fell out with his tutor and after two years, aged ten, ran away. Yichang, still hoping for great things from his son, enrolled Mao with another tutor and, to give him something more practical to do, set him to work on the family and farm accounts. Mao, never with a head for figures, hated the task even more than his school work. Mao's father was incensed and took to beating him.

Mao went on demonstrating that he was no ordinary compliant Chinese son who respected his father. He took to arguing with Yichang and then to flouting his authority, behaviour unheard of in the Chinese heartland of Shaosan. On one occasion he perpetrated the ultimate outrage of rowing with his father in front of guests and then dashing out of the house with his father in pursuit. Mao halted at the edge of the pond and threatened to jump in if his father came any nearer. He liked telling the story in later life, adding that his father backed down. Mao never forgot what he thought of as his father's cruelty, and boasted that if Yichang were still alive he would have had him 'jet-planed,' a form of torture with the head forced down and the arms wrenched behind the back.

In spite of the idyll of his younger years, Mao's experience was following the pattern of Stalin and Hitler, with harsh treatment from the father allied to a doting mother. Harsh treatment handed out to a son by a tough father is a recipe for a damaged ego and damaged male egos are, it seems, a prerequisite for tyrants. But there have been plenty of male children who fell foul of their fathers, and who had doting mothers, but who did not go on to become tyrants. Looking at all three of our tyrant examples it is clear that the ego damage inflicted by their fathers was so severe that it resulted in an insatiable desire not simply to get even with their fathers, but to get even with mankind. They would show their own countrymen who was boss and, if they had half a chance, the world. And anyone who stood in the way would be trampled down.

Stalin and Mao shared one other intriguing attribute. In spite of despising the peasants of their own countries, they deliberately cultivated a brutish peasant manner when dealing with their peers. Both were clever, but were averse to any outward show of intelligence. Stalin was particularly smart at alienating his comrades by his outward coarseness, using this brute persona to disguise from his peers, whom he inevitably saw as rivals, the ways in which he was plotting their downfall. Early on, Stalin showed his daring, organizing ability and ruthlessness, by carrying out the great Tiflis coach robbery, reported worldwide, when his gang attacked those guarding a coach full of money in the main square of the Georgian capital, killing forty and wounding fifty more. The £1.7 million haul went straight into the coffers of the communist party, boosting Stalin's prestige in the party, especially in the eyes of Lenin. The fact that Stalin had seduced and made pregnant a 13 year old village girl just before the revolution counted for nothing compared with his dedication to the cause.

Stalin was notorious for the cruelty he meted out on his own people, especially the rural poor. Most of the twenty million people Stalin is calculated to have killed were peasants and kulaks, the smallholders who owned their own piece of land. Mao hated China's peasants even more. Mao's dream, although in his day unachievable, was to modernize China, and the peasants were the fuel to feed the modernizing machinery. Although Mao's propaganda successfully put over the image of a caring leader, he never wavered in his view that the peasants were totally expendable.

Power not only corrupts tyrants, it makes them deranged. By the time Mao launched the Great Leap Forward in May 1958, he was unhinged, believing that with one great stride China could industrialize and overtake the West. The basis for the much-hyped leap was food production. Mao's despised peasants were to revolutionize agricultural methods and the resulting wheat and rice surpluses exported in exchange for machinery, mainly from Russia. Within a few years, Mao senselessly believed, China would be turned into an industrial powerhouse.

The idea that China could become a superpower overnight was a figment of Mao's deluded mind, yet the peasants had to be sacrificed to the myth. Huge grain yields, from lands named 'Sputnik fields' by Mao, who was obsessed with the Russian satellite, were regularly reported in the press. The yields were imaginary, part of Mao's Great Leap Forward propaganda machine, but the peasants were expected to hand over to the state correspondingly increased amounts of produce. When these extra surpluses were not forthcoming, Mao alleged that the peasants were eating carrot leaves by day and rice at night, an accusation that they were putting on a show of being poorly fed while eating well in secret. By starving the peasants, China was able to export 4.74 million tons of grain in 1959, worth US$935million. Mao had been told in advance by his advisers, in December 1958, that his policies would result in millions of deaths through starvation. It was then that he made his notorious remark, 'Deaths have benefits. They (the dead peasants) can fertilise the ground.'

Mao and Stalin hated their peasants for the same reason. Each dreamt of turning his own country into a superpower. While the lowly peasants existed, they were a hated reminder that their countries were still poor and backward. Hitler had no peasants to act as scapegoats, but he did not need to look far. He had the Jews.

The atrocities of the Tyrant Three are well documented, although the numbers of their victims can only be approximate. Reasonable estimates are that Hitler's policies led to 8 million murdered, Stalin's to 20 million and Mao's to 70 million. These horrifying totals are unlikely to be surpassed. The roughly contemporary reigns of the three mega-tyrants required not only the availability of ego-damaged males with a demonic determination to gain power, it also needed three countries in a state of chaos and near to economic collapse. If a country is in sufficient turmoil, the people will turn to a saviour who gives strong leadership and promises a way out of the disorder. The lesson that perhaps the world has learned after experiencing the traumatic horrors perpetrated by Stalin, Hitler and Mao is the one that Lord Acton taught over a century ago, 'Power tends to corrupt and absolute power corrupts absolutely.'

The emergence of the three great tyrants at about the same time was no coincidence. To make progress, the world, as well as individuals, must get sick of its sickness. The rule of the three great tyrants demonstrated the evils wrought by dictators with unlimited power. The fact that the three great tyrants now appear to us as the last freak dinosaurs of an older and more bestial age is an encouraging sign. We shall not see their like again.

As horrific as the reigns of the Tyrant Three were, there is one worse atrocity than wreaking vengeance on the human race by mass murder for a decade or two. The greater atrocity is achieved by sowing the seeds of hatred and division which ensure that conflict and mayhem take their toll over centuries. The propensity of one country, or those of one political or religious persuasion, to oppose those of another country or sect, as in the Crusades, as in the conflicts between Catholics and Protestants, as in the enmity between Shia and Sunni, is a symptom of the Us and Them phenomenon, a character defect to which males are specially vulnerable.

4

US   AND   THEM

The Us and Them mentality is at the root of all conflict, setting race against race and the members of one religion against another. On a personal level, it creates rifts in families and sets neighbour against neighbour.

The chimpanzee is the closest ape to man's primeval ancestors and how deeply the Us and Them phenomenon is ingrained in man's forebears is apparent from the behaviour of chimpanzee male raiding parties. Periodically a group of male chimpanzees will gather as a fighting group and set off, deliberately and quietly, to the edge of their territory and beyond. What happens next depends on what they find in the neighbouring territory. If the raiding party see a sizeable group of their rivals including males, they will retreat and try another route. If they come across a lone male, the party will stalk him silently, spread out, and then attack. Usually the lone male will be caught and held by a senior heavier male while the others, shrieking in a frenzy, beat and batter the captive until he is unconscious. If there is a weighty rock nearby the attackers may hurl it at the senseless victim as a parting shot before, excited and hooting, they return to their own territory. The injured victim will invariably die.

Chimpanzee males, like human males, indulge in gratuitous violence. The raiders are not hunting for food, more for fun, or at least to find a diversion to satisfy their aggressive instincts. While engaged in the attack they are excited and shouting. It is as if the male chimpanzees every now and then need to let off steam, to give way to some killer instinct that builds up over time until they have to assuage it. The raiding party see themselves and any others of their group as Us. All members of the neighbouring group are Them and fair game for attack.

We can never be sure that primitive man indulged in similar aggression. But the pitched battles between rival football supporters in recent times, the readiness of young males in towns and cities to form rival gangs, the current gun gang shootings among black youths in British big cities, the spate of stabbings by mainly white youths, the late night drunken street fights in any of our towns, all these happenings suggest so.

What we can be sure about is the ease with which humans can be influenced to think in terms of Us and Them. A glaring example a few decades ago was the prolonged antagonism between the unions and British car manufacturers. The unions, under the leadership and thumb of 'Red Robbo' Robinson, were not so much fighting for their rights as to show who was boss. Against the weak management of the time, particularly in British Leyland, the unions established that they were the ones who ruled. Graham Turner, the journalist and writer who camped at the British Leyland factories for over a year researching the subject, concluded that the British Leyland nightshift was simply a huge card school. If any new worker was naïve enough to try to put in some work on the nightshift he was quickly disciplined and brought into line.

Eventually, with some help from Margaret Thatcher, it dawned on British unions, as it had on American and German unions for some time, that companies and workers do better if they think as We rather than Us and Them. Not that this makes unions redundant. The price of benevolent management is eternal vigilance.

The propensity for man to adopt the Us and Them attitude has intrigued psychologists in recent times and it led some years ago to the psychology faculty of Bristol University trying out a novel experiment. A new intake of students was divided randomly into two groups and each group interviewed separately by the lecturer in charge of the experiment. The first group were told that they had been selected because they showed special promise and members of the group were accorded the title of Augustinians. The second group were given a similar story except that they were to be known as Justinians. The staff observed the intake over their first year and found that the rivalry between the two groups was intense. Students who had been friends on arrival but who had been allocated to different groups broke off their friendships. Augustinians would not join student activity groups with Justinian leaders and vice versa. The students had been allocated to their Emperor groups purely at random yet loyalty to the group was instant and irreversible while the groups stayed together.

Arthur Koestler, writer and intellectual, was interested in the Us and Them phenomenon from childhood because of an experience on his first day at school in Athens. On entering the playground he was immediately seized on by a boy a year or two older and asked which football team he supported, Panathinaikos or Olympiakos. Koestler had no interest in sport and had never heard of either team, but his survival instinct came to the rescue and he blurted out Panathinaikos. Koestler was later amused to recall that, although he never took any interest in football or sport in general, when he looked at a newspaper the first thing he did was to look at the sports page to see if Panathinaikos had been playing and if they'd won.

The first and seminal experiment on Us and Them attitudes took place at a summer camp near Robber's Cave, Oklahoma in the 1950's. Twenty two white, Protestant, well adjusted eleven-year old boys were invited to the camp and the psychologists running the experiment split the boys into two groups that were allocated separate quarters. Unlike in the Bristol experiment, the split was not random, since friends were deliberately separated, and at Robber's Cave the groups decided their own titles and special functions. One group, the Rattlers, prided themselves on their toughness and refusal to report or complain about injuries. The other group, the Eagles, made a point of eschewing that common summer camp symptom, celebrated hilariously by Bob Neuhart in his *Dearest Mother, Dearest Father* song parody, homesickness.

After the week or so that the groups took to settle down, a series of events was arranged when teams from each group competed with each other. The first event was a game of baseball. It was played fairly and the Eagles lost. That night, the Eagles organized a sneak raid on their rivals' camp and burned the Rattlers' flag. The next day the groups faced each other and the Rattlers' leader tried to get the Eagles to admit that they had burned their flag. A fight ensued and the psychologists had to step in and calm things down. That night the Rattlers raided the Eagles' camp and then the Eagles retaliated with their own raid, the members of each group now having armed themselves with baseball bats and sticks and carrying stones for use as missiles.

During the ensuing melee the Rattlers stole items from the Eagles' camp and when the Eagles negotiated to get them back, the Rattlers agreed to return them only if the Eagles crawled on their bellies. The cycle of revenge attacks and humiliations would have continued had not the experimenters stepped in and set tasks that could only be accomplished by the two groups working together.

The Robber's Cave experiment was contrived. In their book *Demonic Males*, Richard Wrangham and Dale Peterson describe a real life situation in which three close friends, Art Heyman, Larry Brown and Doug Moe went to North Carolina on basketball scholarships. Although one of them, Art Heyman, was going to a different college, Duke, from the other two, who went to North Carolina, they were all in the same state and intended to keep up their friendship. But by the time the colleges met in a freshman game, the friendship had been ended, Moe spitting at his former friend Heyman. At a game during the next season Brown and Heyman collided and started to fight so furiously that it took ten policemen to separate them.

Group loyalties are strong and irrational. As I write this, a teenage boy at an ice rink in London has been reported killed. According to his fellow school students, it was because his tastes were chav, meaning that he dressed differently and had musical tastes that were not shared by the majority. The Us and Them phenomenon can, at its simplest involve just three people, as when recently a husband and wife, an Us of only two members, were found to have tortured their young child, seen as a single Them, for several years. The parents were, certainly at an unconscious level, aware of the shakiness of their relationship and were able to bond together only as a desperate twosome indulging in taboo behaviour. In their role as joint outsiders who were holding out against a world that would have regarded them as irredeemably depraved, they were able to form some sort of sick union.

The same mechanism was at work in the notorious and well known cases of male serial killers who were aided and abetted by their partners. On a large scale it led to the still scarcely credible horrors of the Holocaust. It explains the Japanese kamikaze fighter pilots in World War II who, believing in a heroic death, flew their aircraft into Allied ships and other targets. It is the explanation for the current spate of suicide bombings by Muslim fanatics.

The term psychologists use for those who indulge in this kind of Us depravity is deindividuation, although coining a new word could have been avoided by using a familiar one, dehumanisation. It is not necessary to go into the psychology of the Us and Them phenomenon. It is enough to be sufficiently aware of the pitfall that we don't fall into the trap ourselves.

It is no use condemning partisanship in others if we indulge in any Us and Them judgements ourselves, no point in condemning the Holocaust and suicide bombings if we think it all right, say, to write off the blacks who are involved with drug and gun crime. By all means hate what they are doing, but love them enough to create a police force that prevents black criminal men, or any other lawless section of society, from perpetrating their atrocities. Love is the only way to create a better world, but love must not be equated with weakness.

The Us and Them phenomenon, like the rest of the world's problems, is essentially a male prerogative. The male ego is more powerful than that of women, more vulnerable and more easily damaged, more inclined to seek vengeance for the perceived hurt. The usual trigger to an Us and Them confrontation requires the men of the Us group to decide that the Them group have transgressed in some way. The transgression can be purely imaginary: that the Thems have made, unheard but assumed, slighting references to the virility of the Us males. Or the actions seen as transgressions can be factual: that the football supporter dressed in his team's colour of blue has provocatively strayed into red territory; that certain women in the village masquerading as healers are indulging in magical and devilish practices; that a loner in Year Four is into heavy metal rather than rap or hip-hop.

These are moderate and fleeting violations for which the Us group males will usually exact only token punishments, a beating up here, a minor stabbing there. Where knife and gun cultures are on the increase, the Us penalty for infringements by Thems is increasingly likely to be a killing.

We have already seen the horrific consequences resulting from ego-damaged males assuming a position of absolute power in our study of the Tyrant Three. However horrific the atrocities perpetrated by tyrants, the violations last only as long as the tyrant reigns. But Us and Them confrontations can continue indefinitely if the seeds sown are poisonous enough. Sunni and Shia have been in conflict for 1400 years, Catholic and Protestant for five hundred. Religious antagonisms arise because they involve attachment to faith and dogma. For man to progress, individuals need to reject Us and Them prejudices, to discard the trappings and dogmas of the old faiths, and to abandon the shibboleth that leadership is the sole prerogative of men.

5

THE INVENTING MEN

The inventiveness of men, whether or not arising as a compensatory mechanism for their inability to bear children, is nevertheless staggering. Only a man would spend his time in the bath trying to solve the tricky problem of whether a crown made for his employer, King Hieron II of Syracuse, was pure gold, as claimed by the crown maker, or alloyed with silver as the king suspected. As we all know, this teaser was solved by the bather in question, Archimedes, who shouted Eureka! 'I have found it,' jumped out of the bath and dashed home - like most Syracusans he bathed in the public baths - naked. He was in a hurry to test out his bath-time inspiration that, since gold was heavier than silver, if immersed in water it would displace a greater amount of the liquid than would a similar volume of silver.

Another eureka moment features Isaac Newton sitting under an apple tree and an apple dropping on his head, the resulting shock leading to his discovery of gravity. Good stories are mostly exaggerated and eureka moment stories more so, and it seems that the facts are more ordinary. The reason that in 1665 Newton went to spend time at his old home was because Trinity, his Cambridge college, closed down on the arrival of the Great Plague (the Black Death was a name for it invented in Scandinavia and adopted here in the 18th Century to distinguish the 1665 plague from the earlier outbreaks). At that stage, Cambridge had no idea that it had witnessed the most remarkable undergraduate career in its history, Newton having confined his unimaginably advanced thinking to his private notebooks.

During the plague-enforced sabbatical at Woolsthorpe, Newton laid down the foundations of the calculus and elaborated his innovative ideas about light and colour and planetary motion. It was while he was at dinner one evening, reading a book by Galileo, that Newton glanced out at the orchard, saw an apple fall, and began to ponder the gravitational force responsible. The more fanciful story is that Newton was sitting under an apple tree at the time and an apple fell on his head, and visitors to Woolsthorpe Manor, off the A1 south of Grantham, are shown the tree, although it is admitted that the original blew down in 1820. After souvenir hunters had stripped the tree, a nine foot length was left and it is from a shoot of this, visitors are assured, that the present tree was grown.

The breadth of Newton's knowledge and the acuity of his brain has probably never been surpassed, but he was crippled emotionally for life by his treatment as a child.
He had a disastrous start, a tiny baby born prematurely and not expected to live. As if this were not enough, his father had died three months before. When Isaac was two he virtually lost his mother Hannah too when she married a well-to-do minister, Barnabas Smith, the couple deciding that Isaac should be raised by his grandmother. It was only when Barnabas died, when Isaac was eleven, that he was able to form a relationship with his mother, but he was already irretrievably damaged. Later he confessed that during the separation from his mother he had threatened Hannah and

Barnabas with burning their house down and them with it.

Widowed a second time, Hannah concerned herself with Isaac and sent him to King's School, Grantham, and after a time brought him home to take over the sizeable farm and estate acquired from her two marriages. Isaac could not have been a less competent estate manager, curling up under a tree with a book when he should have been attending to the cattle. Hannah relented and Isaac went back to school at Grantham where he was competent in Latin, although there is no record of any special aptitude for mathematics.

On matriculation Newton obtained a place at Trinity College, Cambridge and discovered that Cambridge was a scientific backwater, its syllabus based on Aristotelian theorizing even though Copernicus and Galileo had already established the heliocentricity of the solar system. Newton was forward looking and eventually discovered the works of René Descartes based on a mechanical view of the universe composed of particles of matter. In the notebook intended for taking down his course work, Newton wrote, in Latin, 'Plato is my friend, Aristotle is my friend, but my best friend is truth.' From then on Newton pursued his own scientific speculations, culminating in his *Philosphiae Naturalis Principia Mathematica*, usually abbreviated to *Principia*, incorporating the three laws of motion and the properties of gravity, the fundamental basis for the whole of modern science.

Most scientists would have been content with discovering a fraction of the knowledge revealed by Newton, but Newton was never to know contentment. On publication of the *Principia* by the Royal Society in 1686, Robert Hooke, who had earlier, based on intuition, suggested to Newton that the force of attraction between two objects decreases as the square of the distance between them, raised a charge of plagiarism. Hooke's health was already in decline and a generous acknowledgement by Newton would have gracefully closed the matter. Instead, Newton went through the *Principia* manuscript and erased almost all of the references to Hooke. Even that was not enough to vent Newton's fury. He refused to publish his *Opticks* or to accept presidency of the Royal Society until Hooke was dead.

Newton was never able to erase the damage to his psyche received through his mother's and stepfather's rejection of him as a child. Despite national and European acclaim of the *Principia*, Newton sought further proof of success, involving himself in the politics of the day and obtaining, through his friendship with Charles Montagu, later Lord Halifax, the post of warden of the mint that often brought him in - his salary depended on the output of gold and silver coinage - the huge income of £2000 a year. The friendship was not due to a meeting of minds but largely due to Montagu, fat, forty and by no means handsome, becoming infatuated by Newton's niece, Catherine Barton. Newton, although a puritan in sexual matters and celibate himself throughout his life, was ambitious enough to overlook the impropriety, and Montagu and Catherine became lovers.

Fame and money were not enough to assuage Newton's inward hurt and after he became president of the Royal Society in 1703 he used his position to seek out and ruin anyone his paranoid mind suspected of opposing him. Such was Newton's vindictiveness that an impressive portrait of Hooke in the Royal Society's headquarters 'disappeared' soon after Newton's appointment.

For years Newton carried out a running battle with John Flamsteed, the Astronomer Royal, whom he accused of withholding lunar observations necessary for his continuing work on planetary motion. Newton got himself appointed chairman of a board of visitors overseeing the Royal Observatory's work and he used his friend Edmond Halley to seize Flamsteed's records, the fruit of a lifetime's work, and to prepare them for publication. Flamsteed, awarded a court order to prevent publication, burnt the printed sheets and Newton retaliated by removing fifteen references to Flamsteed's work in the *Principia* and pettily attributing the data to the Royal Observatory.

As Newton's feud with Flamsteed waned, he found an even more eminent adversary in Gottfried Leibniz the German mathematician and philosopher who had invented the calculus in 1675 and published his methods in 1684. Newton had preceded him and taught the calculus to his Cambridge students on returning to Trinity College after the Plague closure, but Newton could never accept that Leibniz had made the discovery independently, claiming that Leibniz's attention had been drawn to the calculus by John Collins, a publisher who was aware of Newton's work.

Newton, who dictated to the members of the Royal Society as if they were his minions, got the Society to appoint an 'impartial' committee, hand-picked by him, to report on the question of prior discovery. His paranoia went further and he secretly drafted the findings of the committee, awarding priority of discovery to himself. He even reviewed the committee's findings anonymously in the Society's *Philosophical Transactions*. Newton, supported by his henchmen, continued to hound Leibniz, the feud being Newton's main preoccupation for the last 25 years of his life. Any publication by Leibniz would provoke a furious polemic by Newton against the German, only the latter's death stemming the onslaughts.

Newton, as genius is entitled to be, is revered for his scientific achievements. We no more dilute our regard for him because of his rancour than we let Wagner's anti-semitism cloud our appreciation of his music. Newton, at least in his early years, sought remedies for his inner turmoil and most of his earlier writings were on religious themes. Throughout his life he presented himself as an orthodox Protestant, but privately he nursed dissident opinions, holding the heretical Arian view denying the doctrine of the Trinity for which Arius, the belief's chief early proponent, was excommunicated in 321 and then banished by the first Council of Nicea in 325.

More surprising to his fellow scientists would have been Newton's interest, amounting to an obsession, in astrology and alchemy, but he kept this a close secret.
Newton in fact wrote far more on religion, alchemy and astrology during his lifetime than on science. Alchemy was one of several arcane pursuits that have occupied otherwise sensible participants over the millennia, and was theoretically concerned with turning base metals into gold, although its main attraction was the hope that practitioners would obtain health, wealth and happiness. The former was to be achieved by alchemical medicines - alchemists were always coming up with new elixirs of life - and wealth would result from converting base metals to gold. The happiness, presumably, would result from securing the other two.

Whatever reservations Newton had about Anglicanism, he was required to sign the Thirty Nine Articles of the Anglican Church on the awarding of each of his Cambridge B.A. and M.A. degrees, on the award of his fellowship and a fourth time on his nomination as Lucasian Professor of Mathematics (the post currently held by Stephen Hawking). In those days Cambridge professorships were only awarded to those who had taken holy orders but somehow Newton managed to avoid this requirement.

Newton's interest in alchemy was not that he wanted gold - he was after all an extremely well paid warden of the mint - but he was probably in need of a belief to counter the inner bitterness resulting from his childhood rejections. If that was his hope it was a vain one. Nor could his formidable mind - Newton was described in his time as 'intellectual master of the universe' - bring him inner peace. If knowledge could bring happiness, Newton would have been the most contented man alive. As it was, he never discovered the cure for all human hurts, the love of God.

We live in an age of science and Newton's stature has never been higher. There are lessons to be learned from Newton's life, but the world has not absorbed them. The view of most scientists and that of males generally is that the world needs more Newtons, more scientific discovery, more knowledge. Men, we must remind ourselves, are fascinated by exploration and discovery, have a biological need to find a purpose whether it is venturing into space or trying to replicate the conditions after the Big Bang. Men, those we allow to lead this world, make decisions that give them a sense of purpose, not conclusions that help the greatest number of people. Left to their own devices, men will opt for wars and Star Wars programmes that will bankrupt their nation, and with economic policies based on free market forces and worldwide perpetual growth that can only in the end devastate the planet. The inventiveness of men does not qualify them to run the world. Leadership needs to be caring more than it needs to be clever. Leadership needs the input of mankind's natural carers, the input of women.

The world has enough knowledge. What it needs is wisdom.

6

THE   SEEDS   OF   THE   NEW   DAWN

It is time to explain how what has been written so far came into being.

When I was six years old, a few months after my father had died, I had a vivid dream that has stayed with me all my life. In the dream, I was in a room into which streamed light from an upper window on to an old style printing press. There was nothing else in the room. In the press was a broad sheet of paper and as I looked at its gleaming whiteness I was filled with a feeling of the utmost bliss. A second dream followed, equally vivid, although more down-to-earth, depicting a specific event in a far-off country.

Both dreams remained vividly in my memory but I had no inkling of their significance until I was in my forties when I read and studied Jung and learned something of the importance of dreams. Then it became clear that the dream of the printing press signified that one day I was meant to write something of significance. By then the event in the far-off country, predicted in the second dream, had happened during the time that I lived and worked as a pharmacist in Sarawak. It seemed that I had been given this second dream and its fulfilment as evidence that the first dream would also be realized.

Although most of my working life was spent as a pharmacist, I began to write early on, first for the local English language magazine when I worked in the Far East and later experimenting with writing for television and the stage. I received encouragement from the BBC with a dramatized version of the early life of Jung, but acceptances were few and far between and I found that I had little control over the finished product, and I turned to writing on medical and health matters, mostly for the *Pharmaceutical Journal*.

At the end of 2006, in my late seventies, I felt stirrings that I thought heralded the writing foretold in my childhood dream and I decided to write a book about helping the world, pointing out injustices and suggesting how things could be improved. Both my grandfathers had been lay preachers and saving the world is probably in my genes.

Early in 2007 I wrote some moralizing chapters on the state of mankind and the need for change, and came up with a title, *A Better World*. At the beginning of April I read what I had written and realized that it was pious, trite and boring. I complained to God. I had given up painting, the pastime I loved, to concentrate on writing. My friends were enjoying their gardens and the benefits of retirement while I had been stuck at a keyboard. Was I or wasn't I to write something useful to the world? I was approaching eighty. Surely I ought to be getting on with it?

I awoke in the early hours of 7th April 2007, Easter Saturday, and was compellingly told that the book was to be called *The New Dawn*. At the same time I was filled with the sublimity that I experienced during my childhood dream and a few times since. As the transcendence faded I saw a picture of the future which showed business executives at home talking to their colleagues who appeared as life-size images. I was shown rusting railway lines and office blocks in a large city, perhaps London, empty and being converted into homes. I saw a newspaper placard with a headline: The End of the Great Commute.

There were no more pictures but it was impressed on me that China would figure importantly in the era of the New Dawn.

The next morning I went to the keyboard and wrote like a man possessed. Whereas before I had been wishy washy and earnest, now I was certain and incisive. My usual writing, even when I knew something about the subject, is half a sentence then a stop and revision, then the rest of the sentence and further revision. What I was getting was non-stop. At the end of each morning I could hardly believe what I had written. After writing five chapters I came to a halt. The voice dried up. At this point I went off to Wales with my partner Em, and in the lovely country near Cader Idris I remembered a passage Kipling had written in his autobiography, *Something of Myself*. When his writing flowed effortlessly, Kipling said, he knew he was receiving help from another dimension. He called his helper his Daemon.

I realized that I had received help with the five chapters and because of his didactic style I called my helper the Lecturer. The problem was that when I came to the keyboard after our holiday, the Lecturer was not there. I waited for days without knowing what to write and I felt let down. All I had been given was the title of a book and five opening chapters. It was as if I had been shown the Star in the East and not been given a camel.

7

SAD SIGNS, GOOD NEWS

It is clear that from now on that I am on my own. There are to be no more outpourings of ready-made text from the Lecturer. I have not been abandoned. It is simply that I have to find my own words. In the early hours of this morning I awoke to find myself listing the world's current woes.

Wars were left out. The world, since we became urbanized, has always had wars. But some of the current dilemmas seem peculiarly our own, special to the 21st Century. There has never been wealth on such a scale. In the past wealth was confined to monarchs, barons, the aristocracy and it is a sign of progress that money is now more evenly distributed. Poverty never helped anybody, but it did not preclude happiness. As we are finding, acquiring money does not itself lead to contentment.

A mere century ago we believed that violence was a result of poverty, the reaction of a minority to being deprived. Now affluence has replaced poverty and we know differently. Violence is more usually the prerogative of youths whose reason has been obliterated by cheap alcohol and often drugs. The politicians respond in the only way they can, futilely, by pragmatic measures such as increasing the price of alcohol. The remedy for violence and drug taking is not by means of laws or legislation, but by a change of heart in the perpetrators, by a spiritual awakening.

We are all aware that there are no longer any poor countries. They are all developing ones. The West assumes that those countries in poverty want to emulate the richer and more developed nations and to create urban conglomerates with their inhabitants sitting for part of each day in gridlocked traffic jams. The International Monetary Fund, a well-meaning body of financial experts, provides loans to developing countries providing the funds are used to feed the markets. Where the poor farming family once scratched a living by growing most of their own food – usually with the women doing the hardest work – they are now given a loan to enable them to abandon farming and to produce goods for the market, generating cash with which they can, in theory, have a better standard of living. In practice, it means that when, as is inevitable with economic cycles, there is a fall in the price of the goods they are producing, the family not only has little income but no food.

With an expanding world population and national governments hellbent on growth, the food mountains of wheat and butter are a thing of the past. Food shortages and food price rises are a more likely feature than surpluses in the immediate future and anyone with a patch of land would be wise to turn it into a vegetable plot.

The free market philosophy is the current obsession of the men who run countries, economies, and businesses, and its proponents believe that spending is the panacea that will solve the world's problems. The success of a country is measured by its GDP and rate of economic growth. People are seen as consumers, and personal worth is measured by the amount of material goods they accumulate. In the early hours of this morning, as I was reviewing the state of the world in some anguish, my cares suddenly evaporated. I had been given a few chapters of a book and a title, *The New Dawn*, without much idea of what it meant. Now it was clear. The sad signs all around us are there to bring us to our senses. We need to become sick of our sickness. The sad signs herald a spiritual rebirth.

The New Dawn is to usher in the worldwide realization that richness of life is what matters and not riches. It will be an era when women cease to be sidelined as guest workers and make their full contribution as 50% of the human race.

8

EXPERIENCING,   NOT   BELIEVING

No one can be angry at a fact. To get angry we have to do some interpreting, find some objection associated with the fact.

God exists. That is a fact which gets some people angry. The reason they give for being angry is, they say, that God does not exist and they object to the propagation of lies. Yet they do not object to the statement that the sky is blue, even though that is not a fact but an illusion caused by the phenomenon of free-electron scattering, as deduced by Lord Rayleigh in 1871. Blueness as such does not exist, but is simply a sensation recorded on human retinas and registering in the brain as blueness. Without any humans to look at the sky, it would not be blue at all. Even so, there are many individuals who accept the blueness of the sky as a fact but cannot accept that God exists.

The notion that God exists annoyed the atheist Richard Dawkins so much that he wrote a whole book, *The God Delusion*, to warn people against being conned into believing. The book is a very well argued polemic against religions, much more cleverly expressed than the attempts in this book. Dawkins and his fellow atheists understandably do not believe in God because they have never taken the steps to finding Him. Those who have experienced oneness with God do not have to concern themselves with believing. Experiencing is all that matters.

Dawkins asks why we so readily accept the idea that the one thing we must do if we want to please God is to believe in him. The insistence on believing in God is a characteristic of the old monotheistic man-made religions, Judaism, Christianity and Islam that Dawkins rightly abjures. Many who believe in God are convinced that He created the universe in seven days, or rather six plus a rest day. Or, if they are thoroughgoing fundamentalists, that the whole of the Bible is God's word and that Leviticus chapter 20 is right in calling for the death penalty for cursing one's parents or being homosexual. The God one experiences by going inside oneself would laugh at the idea that He needs people to believe in Him, or in Leviticus. God wants us to be free from dogma, whether it is the dogma of atheism or even the obligation to believe in Him.

Richard Dawkins is the Charles Simonyi Professor for the Public Understanding of Science at Oxford University and one of his main arguments against God is that the overwhelming majority of FRS (Fellows of the Royal Society, the UK's leading scientific institution) are atheists. Since the individuals constituting this overwhelming majority have not attempted to find God, this is a strangely unscientific conclusion. We also know that whenever there has been a scientific breakthrough, the mass of scientists have been opposed to the idea. This has been demonstrated to be the case whenever any great scientific discovery has been made, as when Copernicus propounded heliocentricity (although Aristarchus of Samos had proposed a heliocentric hypothesis in the 3rd century BC and had been similarly disbelieved), right up to Einstein, Hoyle and those currently speculating on whether there are ten, eleven or twenty seven dimensions of time. Einstein in turn could never come to terms with the indeterminacy principle relating to subatomic particles proposed by Werner Heisenberg. As Thomas Kuhn has so elegantly and conclusively argued in *The Structure of Scientific Revolutions*, scientists stay within the accepted paradigms of the time until they are forced out of them by new evidence. Science is not the whole truth. It is the version that scientists are believing at the time.

The great majority of scientists and atheists will not make the simple experiment of attempting to find God because their minds are closed to the possibility. The experiment requires the adoption of a spirit of enquiry, precisely as is required for a scientific experiment, and the stilling of the mind. This requires practice but can be achieved by anyone undertaking one of the accepted meditation techniques, followed by listening with an open mind. It will help if a spiritually enlightening book such as *A Course In Miracles* is read before or after meditating. Atheist scientists ought to feel secure that they will encounter nothing during the experiment to change their minds. The fact that they do not undertake the experiment suggests that they fear they might.

Scientists accept that they have to go looking for the truth. Heliocentricity did not present itself to scientists, any more than did natural selection or quantum mechanics. Copernicus, Darwin and Planck spent decades searching in their chosen fields. With much less effort, scientists, like anyone else, could find God.

Richard Dawkins and atheists in general consider a belief in God to be a crutch for people who do not feel self-reliant. That does not apply to every believer but as far as I am concerned they are absolutely right. When I tried living my life without God, I, or rather my ego, put on a show of self-confidence and self-reliance. In reality, I was a cork bobbing on the sea of life, at the mercy of the ungovernable waves around me.

The question then arises, is God only for wimps, only for those who feel inadequate? One can only answer this by pointing to examples of those who have experienced God and who do not appear to be in that category. Jesus, to the unbiased, appears to be a complete individual who persuaded many of those he encountered that they could live a fuller life. By all accounts, Saint Paul and Saint Augustine appear to have been men of positive action rather than in need of psyche-bolstering. Joan of Arc was fearless and inspirational. Florence Nightingale heard God's voice a few months before her seventeenth birthday and went on to revolutionise nursing and hygiene. The list could be expanded, but atheists may choose not to be convinced. The most telling argument in favour of God is that no one who has experienced oneness with Him has ever doubted again.

When I think of an example of someone who experiences God, who is guided by compassion, is wise and lives joyfully and in peace, I always turn to His Holiness the Dalai Lama. He has the weight of the world on his shoulders. His homeland is occupied and oppressed. He strives for the liberation of Tibet, refusing to give way to bitterness or to seek retaliation. He smiles and he laughs away the sorrows, sure signs of experiencing God. The lovely irony is that, as a Buddhist, the Dalai Lama does not believe in God. Yet without doubt, he experiences Him. As does anyone who knows freedom and joy.

9

WAYS TO GOD

There are many ways to God. For millennia, individuals have found their way to God through the monotheistic religions, Judaism, Christianity and Islam. It is difficult to assess how many have been put off finding God by acts perpetrated in the name of those faiths. Buddhism and Jainism deny that there is any God but, with a nice irony, pursue well defined practices that are a surer way to finding the God within than the vaguer precepts offered by the monotheistic doctrines.

There is no need here to recount the travesties of religion that have resulted from manipulation of the essences of Christianity and Islam by men, many of them well-meaning, out of fear that the original message would not survive without the help of burning stakes and judicious stonings. It is self-evident that the traditional monotheistic edifices are crumbling in the face of an educated and critical world. Christianity's decline is presided over by shrinking congregations, mainly of the elderly, in churches that are no longer financially viable, apart from the great cathedrals visited in droves by those interested in the architecture. Recruits to Islam are now mainly disaffected young men who are looking for a purer path than the West shows them or than is practiced by their wealthier brethren in the oil-rich Islamic states.

However, because of the events of recent years - I am writing this on 11th September 2007 - a word about Islam might be in order. It so happens that for five and a half years I lived in a country in the Far East where the main religion was Islam and where the majority of those working for me were Muslim Malays. At the time, fifty years ago, I was impressed by the calm dedication of my Muslim staff. On the occasions when expatriates were invited into the Muslim villages, as during the great celebrations to mark the end of Ramadan, one could not help being aware of the remarkable air, pervading even the party atmosphere, of tranquillity and calm.

It is difficult now to equate my experience with the current phenomenon of Muslims blowing up innocent civilians in the countries in which they are living. Islam has always been a paradox. Islam means surrender in the sense of surrendering to God and it is on one hand a simple faith of desert people based on the Qur'an, on the other a religion of differing and often warring sects and of complex beliefs. The one uniting factor for all Muslims is the Qu'ran, the written record of the revelation received by the Prophet Muhammad during the 23-year period from 610 to 632 AD, regarded by Muslims as the direct word of God.

Muhammad had begun taking month-long annual retreats for quiet contemplation in a cave on Mount Hira and it was on his fifth retreat, when he was forty, that he first saw the Angel Gabriel and was commanded to read. Muhammad replied that he could neither read nor write. Gabriel repeated the injunction and explained that the Lord was to teach man what he knew not. Muhammad found the experience deeply unsettling and talked about the experience with his wife Khadijah, who reassured him and encouraged him to accept the validity of his experience, thereby becoming the first person to embrace Islam.

Muhammad received the text in oral form and the words were taken down by a number of scribes. The Qu'ran is studied in conjunction with the Sirah, the story of Muhammad's life. The Qu'ran is addressed to all of humanity, although it is stressed that is intended for 'people who think'. Its readers are repeatedly asked to observe, reflect and question.

.

In Mecca, after Muhammad's first revelation, the Prophet and his followers went through a hard time. Boycotted by most of the city's populace, they took refuge in an outlying suburb where sympathetic relatives secretly supported them. Their hardships were severe and in 616 both the Prophet's wife Khadija and his uncle Abu Talib died. Khadijah had been Muhammad's only wife, but after her death he remarried several times, eleven women in all, one being Jewish and another a Coptic Christian, although both converted to Islam before marriage. The continued persecution in Mecca led the Prophet to visit Taif and after his return he had the vision known as the Miraj during which he had the experience of ascending into heaven. The Prophet then laid down the rule of five daily prayers as the way of worship for Muslims.

The scribes who took down texts received by Muhammad were meticulous in dating the time of each message and Muhammad had to wait three years after the original message from the angel Gabriel before being given further texts. In the meantime Muhammad agonized and only gradually accepted the enormity of the idea that he had been chosen for the revelation. When Muhammad did take the step of going beyond passing his message to a few friends and relatives and started to proclaim Islam, there was a renewed outcry and fierce opposition from the powerful polytheistic Quraysh clan based around Mecca.

In 616 Muhammad was so concerned at the mounting opposition to his teachings that he advised some of his followers to emigrate to Abyssinia and to seek refuge under its Christian leader, the Negus. Eighty Muslims made the journey, including the Prophet's daughter Ruqaiya and her husband Othman bin Affan, who was later to become the third Caliph in succession to the Prophet. The Negus gave the Muslim band his protection and refused the demand by two emissaries from the opposing Quraysh clan for their expulsion.

By 622, the opposition to Islam in Mecca was so great that Prophet decided to leave the city. Small groups of Muslims started to make their way north to the town of Yathrib (later changed to Medina) at the invitation of the citizens who accepted Muhammad as the leader of the new order. The Meccans, far from expressing relief at getting rid of the hated Muslims, became concerned that Islam was spreading and vowed to assassinate the Prophet, who went into hiding. The migration from Mecca, the *Hijra*, is regarded by Muslims as the start of the new era and a Muslim calendar was introduced from that date, 16th July 622 in the Julian calendar.

Although Muhammad fought three battles against the Meccans, these only occupied one month of the ten year Medina period. In 630 Muhammad led a force of ten thousand and marched on Mecca and the city surrendered without a fight. When the Meccan elders were brought to him, Muhammad asked them what they expected of him and, before they could answer, he added that all their crimes were forgiven and that they could go, free of blame.

This event illustrates again the paradox of Islam, with the Prophet himself demonstrating that Allah is merciful, but also that warfare is legitimate. Before we draw conclusions, we should remember the Crusades. However, it is undeniable that the Qu'ran condones violence, with passages that have much in common with the Old Testament, which is revered, along with Abraham and Moses, by Muslims. Just one example will do: 'But the infidels who die unbelievers shall incur the curse of God, the angels, all men. Under it they shall remain forever, their punishment shall not be lightened, nor shall they be reprieved.'

Critics of Islam cite these condemnatory passages from the Qu'ran and argue that they account for the violence of Al Qu'aeda and Muslim suicide bombers. They may as well argue that the Crusades were inspired by the bellicose exhortations of the Old Testament. Wars and violence are perpetrated by men with destructive egos. Some happen to be Muslim, some Christian and others, like Genghis Khan and Mao Tsetung, atheists.

A recent survey showed that over a third of Muslim young men in Bradford, West Yorkshire, believed that the death penalty was the appropriate punishment for those who converted to another religion. Islam has suffered as much from that distortions of its guardians as has Christianity, and the idea that any Muslim who changed his religion should be killed is found not in the Qu'ran, but in the *hadith*, the traditions and sayings attributed to the Prophet by later commentators. Some were well-meaning, but there were inevitably others, the Religion Men, who feared that the rules needed stiffening if the religion was to survive. Extreme views, whether Muslim or Christian, have nothing to do with the religion's founder, but everything to do with the deranged egos of the Religion Men who seek and usually obtain influence and power.

It is these fanatics, Arab terrorists who distort Islam, who are responsible for the Arab-Israeli conflict. Because the Israeli army is well equipped and trained and we see newsreels of Arab youths reduced to throwing stones at Israeli tanks, many of us outsiders believe the Arabs in Palestine are oppressed. In reality, the Arab stone throwers and rocket firers are victims of an Us and Them situation fostered by their ego-crazed leaders. The truth of the situation was encapsulated in two sentences by Benjamin Netanyahu: 'If the Arabs put down their weapons today, there would be no more violence. If the Jews put down their weapons today, there would be no more Israel.' That is not to imply that Israel is blameless. Its illegal occupation of the West Bank is the result of their hardline Religion Men clinging to irrelevant Old Testament dogma.

To understand is to forgive. But that does not mean that the West should be soft on terrorism, whether planned or perpetrated by Muslims or those of any other extremist belief. We need to be eternally vigilant. However, those who argue that the activities of today's Muslim extremists are worse than anything perpetrated by Christians might like to put themselves in the shoes of the Incas and the Aztecs during the time of the conquistadors. They watched their peoples being butchered on a scale not seen until Stalin's purges of the kulaks and Hitler's holocaust. To those who say that the accounts of the bloodshed and torture in the name of Christianity were exaggerated it is enough to point out that the victims had no written language. All the records we have of the torture and slaughter were compiled by the conquerors.

Those who claim that suicide bombers are the inevitable outcome of passages in the Qu'ran have to ignore the centuries when Islam presided over the only civilized parts of the world, with Muslim scholars translating and reviving the classical thought of Greece and Rome and advancing mathematics, chemistry and medicine. During the time of the Islamic ascendancy, from the 7th to the 12th Centuries, Jewish communities enjoyed greater toleration than at any time before or since. It is true that Islam has descended from its days of glory, but then so has Christianity. It is also true that for their religions to have any hope of survival, Muslims and Christians will need to abandon whole rafts of traditional thought and practice. All things, including religions, are subject to change, and change for good is facilitated by difficulties.

Whether any traditional religion will survive the technological age is unclear and need not concern us. Even in a world disillusioned with religion, God is not going to be thrown out with the bath water of religious dogmatism. He is in the hearts of every one of us.

NEW DAWN WOMAN

In the early hours of 7th April 2007 I was told with urgency that the title of the book I was writing should be *The New Dawn*. For weeks there came an outpouring of words and I came to realize that I had been given a message to spread, a whole new book. I was given help. First came the Lecturer, who bombarded me with text and the reader with erudition. Then I was left to my own resources, or at least that was what I thought. In fact, I realize now, I was given subjects connected with the New Dawn to include, although by a more gentle mentor than the Lecturer, a guide who gave hints rather than taking over.

During the time it took to write the first chapters of this book I viewed the New Dawn as a future event. Naively, I thought that God was relying on my book to announce the message to the world, to get it started. There were times when I wondered if I was up to the job, if the New Dawn would ever happen. Always, in writing this book, whenever I have had doubts or misinterpretations they have been removed by evidence that I could not miss. This morning I was shown that the world did not have to wait for my book, that the New Dawn has already started, is already brightening the skies, heralding a time of unprecedented hope. The evidence, not surprisingly, is provided by a woman. Remarkably, she lives in Kabul, the capital of Afghanistan.

Westerners on the whole deplore those Muslim countries where male regimes impose the wearing of coverings by women. The burqa comes in for special criticism, being an enveloping head-to-toe garment with veiled eyeholes that completely obscures the identity of the wearer. However, for Malalai Joya, the burqa is the key to freedom. Wrapped in its anonymity she moves around Kabul, inspiring hope among its women and exposing the corrupt practices of Afghanistan's male parliamentarians and ministers, the leaders supported by the American and British governments.

Malalai Joya came to prominence in 2003 when she was elected to Afghanistan's newly established national assembly, the Loya Jirga, in her home province of Farah. During her first appearance in the assembly, on 17th December 2003, Joya rocketed into controversy by demanding that the country's fundamentalist warlords, criminals and drug traffickers should not only be banned from any role in Afghanistan's future but that they should be tried as war criminals. This was too straight and to-the-point for the predominantly male and cronyist chamber and, after refusing to apologise or to retract her accusations, the security guards were called and she was ejected. The aggressive and chauvinist male Muslim power base in Afghanistan now had her in their sights. Joya was a marked woman.

To Afghan women and the country's oppressed poor, Joya became a beacon of hope and in September 2005, aged 27, she was elected as the Farah representative to the national parliament. Her male establishment enemies got out their knives and did not have to wait long. Joya was no sooner in parliament than she was publicising her views to fellow members, journalists and human rights groups. They may now be wearing suits and ties, she declared, but the country's leaders were still the same corrupt, greedy, murderous warlords and religious fundamentalists who had brought about the country's ruin.

As a child, Joya witnessed the horrors of the Taliban regime. The Taliban were fanatical in their oppression of women. They ruled that girls could not be educated beyond the age of eight, that women were not allowed to work, nor be treated by male doctors. It was the Taliban who decreed that no woman could appear in public without the burqa. Joya raged against the men who dictated what women should wear, but now that the Taliban tyrants have gone from Kabul, she uses the burqa to ensure anonymity and the continuance of her work helping the girls and women who lived through the nightmare of Taliban rule. Joya is tireless in her determination to publicly expose those responsible.

As with most brave and outspoken individuals, Joya is not careful of her own safety. Given a television interview in May 2007 Joya denounced the legislature, claiming they were 'worse than a zoo'. An edited recording of the interview was shown in parliament and her male enemies got her ejected from parliament, citing violation of a rule of procedure that forbids lawmakers to criticise one another.

Joya is well aware that the Afghanistan male establishment wants her dead and that there is a price on her head. Her response is hugely courageous. 'They will kill me, but they will not kill my voice, because it will be the voice of all Afghan women,' was her answer early in 2007 to the death threats. 'You can cut off the flower, but you cannot stop the coming of spring'.

Joya has not completely rejected Islam, although she acknowledges that many crimes have been committed in its name. She describes herself as a secular Muslim, and has always resisted the idea that Muslim men should dominate their women and decide what Muslim women should wear. Joya's father wanted to be a doctor but in his teenage years Afghanistan was in the pre-Taliban turmoil of the Jihad, the ' holy war' against the Russian occupiers, and he became a freedom fighter instead of a medical student. In the fighting Joya's father lost part of his leg and the family became refugees, first in Iran, and then in Pakistan, ending his hopes of becoming a doctor.

It was while Joya was in the refugee camp that she was contacted by representatives of an underground campaign group, OPAWC (the Organisation for Promoting Afghan Women's Capabilities) and realized that she could serve the cause of Afghan women and at the same time earn some desperately needed cash. The work was all underground and dangerous and Joya was obliged to buy and wear one of the hated burqas. Her brothers were astonished, and laughed at seeing their firebrand sister dressed in the garment that she had described as 'a shroud for the living' and as the symbol of women's oppression, but it gave Joya the anonymity she needed to carry on her work covertly teaching the women of Herat to read and write. Even in the burqa, Joya feared capture on the streets of Herat by male fanatics working for the Taliban's dreaded Vice and Virtue Department. Sometimes she was obliged to knock on the door of a strange house and ask for a drink and to be taken in to avoid their patrols.

Joya, who has been banned from taking her seat in parliament until 2009, now works under cover in Kabul. Glyn Strong, one of the first Western reporters to interview Joya, wrote that when his rendezvous with Joya had been arranged he was expecting to meet a messianic and frighteningly focused politician. He was met by a tiny, softly spoken, beautiful woman and invited to sit with her on the floor of one of the many 'borrowed' houses she works from. Joya is married but says little about her husband out of fear for his safety.

Joya gives support to the women of Kabul who have suffered from the male-induced violence in recent decades. At one of the secret shelters for women that houses the victims of early forced marriages, abduction and violence in various forms, Strong met Alya and remembers her vividly. Now 16, Alya was bartered into a loveless marriage at 12. When she baked what her husband and mother-in-law regarded as a bad batch of bread she was beaten and had hot oil thrown on her. In desperation, at the prospects of a life of torture, Alya set fire to herself, a not uncommon solution for young girls condemned to a marriage of abuse and torture. Where her hands were there are now only stumps. She cannot feed herself or comb her hair. Alya's plight moves Joya to tears and she apologises for showing her weakness.

But Joya's presence offers hope. Alya wants only three things: a divorce, to have new hands and to get an education. With the inspiration of Joya behind her, one feels that these wishes, even in Kabul, could possibly be realized for Alya. The task ahead for Joya is hard. One in three Afghan women experience violence. The infant mortality rate is 165 per 1000 live births, compared with seven per 1000 in the USA. Every day, on average, 44 Afghan women – many are young teenagers - die giving birth. 87% of Afghan women are illiterate. 80% face forced marriages.

Joya lives the life of an ascetic. She is a vegetarian and carries with her only a small bag containing a book and a radio and a few odds and ends. She never sleeps in the same house for more than one night. She can only move dressed in her burqa and with several volunteer armed male guards. Her husband lives 600 miles away and Joya and they meet infrequently. While the battle for women's freedom in Afghanistan is on she will not have children and may never have them. She realizes that for her husband this is difficult and has offered him a divorce. He agreed to the arrangement to postpone children before their marriage and so far has accepted it.

Joya acknowledges that the American, British and other UN forces in Afghanistan are preventing outright civil war. But America's support for Afghanistan's corrupt leaders make her angry. She says accusingly that President Bush talks about education, but that the fundamentalists in power are burning schools. She is bitter that the expatriate forces believe they are supporting women's right when the reality is that Afghan women are committing suicide because of male violence. She sums up her prescient view: '........ I believe that no nation can donate liberation to another nation. Democracy, human rights, women's rights are not something that someone gives to us. We must ourselves make sacrifices to achieve these values'.

That most of what is wrong with the world is due to male dominance and failed male leadership has so far been overlooked by most women. In April 2007, completely unexpectedly, I was told of a new era, the New Dawn, and that I was to announce its imminence in a book. The story of Malalai Joya showed me that the New Dawn is not waiting for or reliant upon my book, but that it is already on its way. There are women, and some men, who are already working for a new order in which men contribute but do not dominate, and in which women play their full part. The future, despite what we see in the world, is full of hope.

11

THE NEW DAWN

On holiday in Norfolk in the early hours of this morning, 5th July 2007, I awoke in the state of bliss I first knew in my childhood dream, and was given the message of the New Dawn:

The purpose of this life is the giving and receiving of love.

As I came down to Earth, back to my unsure and doubting self, I wondered if that was all there could be to it. One sentence? Just love?

I became submerged by doubt. The world would laugh. People going about their work and daily routines would tell me to get real. Those ensuring that water comes out of the tap, that electricity is available when we press a switch, that the crops are grown and harvested, would tell me that I depended on their labours to indulge in the luxury of my fancy thoughts. That they are too busy providing the essentials to have time for such whimsy.

But I knew in my heart. Thoughts coming in that transcendent state are only ever true. Love is the only element that existed before our life here and will continue ever afterwards. The love we give and receive here is the only meaningful aspect of life. All the material goods and accumulations we acquire count for nothing. All the energy and effort we put into acquiring things is meaningless. Yet every loving thought and act resonates forever.

I was told about the coming of the New Dawn without knowing what it meant. Now I know. With the New Dawn there is no cult, no guru, no dogma. Only love. It is the awakening of individuals to the truth that the giving and receiving of love is all that matters, all that there is to life.

12

HORROR   AND   HOPE

A businesswoman is sitting in a hut in Cambodia, although it could be almost any Asian country, and is bargaining with the mother of the house. Except that the hut is too ramshackle to be called a house. At the end of the bargaining, the mother calls out 'Srey!' and her beaming bright-eyed daughter comes into the hut. Srey's mother tells her that she will accompanying her 'auntie' to the city for a short while. She is to do as she is told and she will return home in a few months.

Srey does not like the made-up woman called auntie, but she is obedient and leaves her home with the clothes she stands up in and her favourite rag doll. Three days later, in a tawdry area of Phnom Penh, Srey finds herself in a seedy brothel. Her eyes are made up with mascara, her lips are vividly reddened, and she is dressed in a purple sarong. She is eleven years old. There is no escape. Srey is handed over to a portly Japanese businessman who takes her virginity and submits her to brutal degradation over five days. He has paid the brothel keeper $500, the same amount that Srey's mother received for selling her into prostitution.

Srey is terrified, but to no avail. Her body from then on is made available to American, British and German sex tourist paedophiles at $10 a time. After a few weeks, Srey has lost most of her value and is worth only $2 a customer, mostly Cambodians and Thais. One thing her mother told Srey was true. She returned home in three months. The reason was that her body, racked with gonorrhoea and HIV, was no longer saleable. She was sent home to die.

Bacia is a teenage African girl, unsure of her exact age. Bacia's country, like many in Africa, is a battlefield between government forces and rebels who call themselves freedom fighters. When rebel forces swept into Bacia's village, she and her family took refuge in a nearby church. The soldiers broke down the church door and Bacia and her father fled into the forest. She has never seen her mother and brothers since.

The soldiers caught up with Bacia and told her to stay with her father, and that reassured her. But not for long. The fathers were at gunpoint told to rape their daughters. Those who refused, including Bacia's father, were shot dead in front of their children. The daughters were then made to dance on their fathers' dead bodies, while the soldiers drank and laughed. Bacia saw the soldiers casually slashing the face of a man who was tied to a tree. They gouged out his eyes. He was still alive. While the soldiers were distracted, a woman grabbed Barcia's hand and they fled into the forest. Soldiers caught up with them and raped them.

Bacia was taken to a house which held five other girls. Gangs of soldiers passed through, raping every girl repeatedly. Bacia was so badly mutilated that for a time she could not walk. After several months of this torture, Bacia was out one day buying food for the soldiers when she was recognized by a man from her village who hid her in his house. Bacia eventually made her way to Britain, but she arrived with no money and no friends. Bacia wandered around the airport until she heard a woman speaking her language and this woman helped her to get a room in a hostel. It was then, having time to think, that the full horror of what she had been through came flooding back. Bacia was almost overwhelmed, but her inner resources held out and carers are helping to restore her to some sort of normality.

The third story concerns a 12 year old Indian girl called Phusi who lived with her parents in a village a few miles from Jaipur in Rajasthan. Phusi was desperate to go to school four miles away but her parents were poor and could not afford to buy her a bicycle. Phusi nagged and cajoled her mother until one day, in a fit of rage, her mother beat her unconscious with the rolling pin used for making chapattis. Fearing she had killed the child, she put a rope round Phusi's neck and hung her body from a ceiling rafter, then rushed outside shouting that her daughter had committed suicide.

Phusi's mother later confessed to the crime and in court her husband explained in mitigation that they had borrowed 28,000 rupees (£350), a small fortune in India, to pay for medical treatment when, after Phusi's birth, her mother had developed complications. In debt for such a sum, the parents could not afford a bicycle for Phusi.

In an ironic aftermath to the story of Phusi, the local state government later announced a scheme whereby all school-age girls would be given a free bicycle to enable them to get to school. However, the bicycles never arrived at Phusi's village.

These stories remind us that atrocities are perpetrated as a result of the power wielded by men. Men use the power of money to indulge their sexual obsessions. Men with political authority use their power to send armies to do their bidding. Men with influence and money entice the naïve to carry drugs to enable them to make more money and to blight the lives of those ignorant enough to adopt a drug habit. Men intent on making money are responsible for clearing the world of its rainforests to produce the wood shuttering used in erecting concrete buildings. There is nothing wrong with erecting new buildings. There is nothing wrong with making money. But we can no longer leave decision making to that small proportion of half of the human race that has proved it cannot on its own be trusted with power

Men do not need stripping of power, but they do need to share it. So far women have not wanted power enough to take on its burdens, but the consequences of leaving power in the hands of men have been staring us in the face for long enough. The New Dawn is issuing in an era when women will use their voice to bring about order, love and peace.

THE VISION

That summer, around the time of my sixth birthday, my father had got hold of a load of sand for me to play with and had piled it on the baked patch of earth that, until that blazing hot summer, had been our small back lawn. I moulded a hill from the sand and assembled the toy castle I had bought, piece by piece, from Woolworths on the tram trips my mother and I took into Leicester every Saturday afternoon. I was allowed a penny to spend and each week I bought a toy soldier. When I had enough soldiers I needed a castle, but these cost three shillings and sixpence, a fortune beyond our reach. But Woolworths cleverly sold sections of the walls, the towers, keep and drawbridge separately at sixpence each and eventually my mother had given in.

I had scooped out a moat around the castle and arranged one lot of soldiers, mostly longbowmen, around the battlements, to defend the fort against the attacking force of Roman legionaries. I had just finished my first year at school and my history was hazy and mostly gained from comic weeklies. The legionaries, I realized, with their short swords and shields could not stage much of an attack against a fort with its drawbridge up, and I had to go back to Woolworths for a Roman catapult to bombard the fort with pebbles.

Outside the fort I modelled the sand into hillocks and streams, made gravel roads that crossed the streams by matchbox bridges, and with twigs from the hedge created a wood where the Romans had their military headquarters. It was on one of those sun-drenched days when I was immersed in the siege operations, exhilarated by the smell of the baked earth and sand, that it happened. I gradually became aware that the excitement of the campaign had given way to stillness, that the bricks and mortar world around me had evaporated and I had expanded infinitely beyond my body. I was somewhere and yet everywhere, part of every being, part of every twig and pebble, every grain of sand. I was in heaven, one with all of creation, full of wonder and joy. And at utter peace.

'Ray, it's dinner time.' My landing back on Earth was soft enough. I even managed to eat a little. My mother thought my lack of appetite was due to the heat. It never occurred to me to tell her about the experience. I would not have known how. Only in later life did I realize that for perhaps thirty seconds I had known the ineffability of being at one with God.

I would like to be able to say that this experience sustained and spurred me on during my life as a seeker, but in fact it has only become meaningful to me during my later years. Last night, after thinking about my childhood experience, during my nightly reading of *A Course in Miracles* I came across a passage I had not read before:

'Sometimes a teacher of God may have a brief experience of direct union with God. In this world, it is almost impossible that this endure.'

It dawned on me that as a small boy, before the world closed in, I had been given a foretaste of life in heaven, of what it is like after we leave the body, and a reminder of what it is like for every one of us in the spirit realm before we take the decision to live in an Earth body.

This is not a common occurrence during our Earth life for the simple reason that after experiencing union with God, the remembrance of it would make life down here unbearable. In my own case, the memory was kept in the background for most of my life so that I could experience the rocky road and the pitfalls that all seekers have to go through to find the truth. Only now, seeing, after so long being blind, am I able to share the experience with others.

14

A   NEW   NAME   AT   DAWN

For some weeks the voice has been badgering me. I would have to publish this book under another name, since my surname, of French origin, is not easily transliterated into Chinese, Arabic or many other languages. The Chinese take a lot of trouble to find a Chinese transliteration of foreigners' names, choosing a flattering one if they can, and when I worked in Hong Kong soon after qualifying as a pharmacist, my Chinese colleagues worked hard on mine. They came up with a contrived name of four syllables that did not flow easily off the tongue and had no auspicious meaning. Disappointment showed in their faces when they told me. The Chinese like to please.

I toyed with pen-names in recent weeks but I could tell that I had not found the intended one. At around 4 o'clock this morning, 20th August 2007, the subject returned and a jumble of syllables came into my mind. I tried to form names out of the mixture but came up with only risible combinations. Then my mind stilled and I heard the word Soweto. But I could not have heard aright. The suggestion that I take the name of a black township in South Africa known for its poverty and sprawl was sillier than any of my attempts. The voice persisted. Soweto, Soweto.

I calmed down. Soweto would transliterate into Chinese as So-Way-To, although whether this was propitious I had no way of knowing. Soweto is a name familiar to many people in all continents. Soweto is known for its community spirit, the community spirit that existed among the urban poor in most countries until it was eroded by affluence. Would it be so terrible to be associated with a community renowned not for its skyscrapers and wealth but for its courage and enterprise in the face of adversity?

I had doubted needlessly. The voice has always guided me aright. I would be glad to see Soweto on the cover of this book.

15

GROWTH – DEATH

'The Earth is our gracious host'. These words struck me to the core. They were spoken by former Jain monk Satish Kumar, who has lived on Dartmoor for 40 years. Kumar was introducing a nature programme on television on the wonders of the plant and animal life on his adopted Devon moorland. His manner was beneficent and his words, by their very gentleness, were a reminder of man's relationship with nature that, in our scramble for material goods, we have largely lost. The Earth is undoubtedly our gracious host, but we have long since stopped behaving as its gracious guests.

Kumar is the founder of the Resurgence Trust, a body that encourages the finding of the right and natural tempo for contemporary living. Fast is connected with quantity, says Kumar, and slow leads to quality. By going slow you may achieve less, but you will achieve better. What all seekers find is that in stillness there is healing.

For the first time, there is on this planet a species that is capable of exterminating itself. Man, led by the small proportion of misguided males who wield power, has forgotten its place in nature. We are in danger of forgetting that we are part of nature, so intent are we on ruling it. We are losing sight of the fundamental fact that we are one with the natural world. We are intent on ignoring the truth that we are just one of nature's myriad species, insanely believing that we can harness nature to the runaway juggernaut of limitless consumerism.

We are wrong. We need all that nature has to offer, from bacteria to the giant trees of the rain forest. We are dependent on nature's bounty, yet we are behaving as if we were a super species to whom nature's laws do not apply. The largest consumer of the world's resources , the United States, uses up the Earth's reserves at a rate equivalent to six Earth-size planets. This rate of consumption could only ever be temporary and only while there existed one superpower. Soon the United States will be joined by China as a super-consumer, and India is not far behind.

The world's national and business leaders are obsessed with economic growth, as if this can somehow be achieved without exhausting the planet's resources. This policy, unless checked, will bring shortages and catastrophe. It is a policy of Growth-Death. Food shortages are already on the horizon. The first riots over higher food prices in Africa have just been reported. The world will need to listen to the voices of the followers of the New Dawn, to accept the realization that love, peace and joy are available to all, and that the consumption and accumulation of material goods, far from satisfying our inner needs, are devouring the resources of the planet that we should be treating as our gracious host.

16

THE TESTAMENT OF THE NEW DAWN

Since 7th April last year I have been awaiting clarification of the New Dawn. I was told, on 5th July 2007, that the message was the giving and receiving of love. That is the essence of the New Dawn, but I knew that the world needed to be told more than that. In the early hours of this morning, 13th January 2008, I was given the following.

The purpose of this life is to recognize God within ourselves and every human being, to give and receive love, and to experience the freedom and joy of realising that we are not bodies but free and eternal spirit entities created by God.

The world is sick because most people have lost their connection with God. God came to be associated with the man-made religions of the last two thousand years and as these religions have been increasingly rejected, so has God. Jesus and Muhammad came to awaken in us the realization of God but their message has become lost in a maze of man-made creeds and dogma. If you are a Christian and believe that you should convert Protestants to Roman Catholicism or vice versa, from Baptists to Mormons, from Seventh Day Adventists to Jehovah's Witnesses, then you have missed the point of Jesus's message. If you are a Muslim and believe you should converts Shias to Sunnis or vice versa, from Ismailis to Wahabis, then you have missed the point of the Prophet's message. God is not to be more readily found in one man-made sect than in another. He is in every one of us, as individuals, and we, as individuals, are one with God and every other.

If you believe, as a Christian, that you are nearer to God than a Muslim or if, as a Muslim, you believe you are nearer to God than a Christian, then you have been deceived by some man-made falsehood. God is one and indivisible.

If you are an agnostic or an atheist, you have seen how religions have behaved in the world and, understandably, doubt God's existence. What you have not yet tried is meditating in peace and tranquillity and allowing the world to recede. God is the essence of every individual, regardless of what beliefs we hold, and will reveal Himself in contemplation. You can of course continue to refuse to see or acknowledge God, but that is as pointless as a clay pot doubting the existence of the potter. The rewards of working with God rather than against Him are so huge and real, the peace experienced so indescribable, that to ignore them is to deny yourself a life richer than you ever imagined.

There are only two emotions, love and fear. Love is the medium in which we are naturally meant to operate. What stops us is the ego's fear. The ego is the idea we have of ourselves, gradually built up as a defence against a world we see as hostile, and added to at each successive bruising encounter. Because the ego is a response to perceived hurts, it is negative and fearful. Whenever you are disappointed, it is the ego that registers the disappointment. Whenever you are angry, it is your ego that registers the anger. Whenever you blame someone else for your life not being perfect, it is the ego who apportions blame.

The attainment of peace and happiness is automatic once you have disbanded the ego. I know because for most of my life I was ruled by the demands my ego made on me. I then came across a book, *A Course In Miracles*, which explained the tyranny of the ego and showed how this could be ended. Under the influence of the ego I had encumbered myself with a whole cartload of burdens like envy at the achievements of others, sensual gratification rather than pleasure, smart thinking rather than knowledge. The realization that these were the ego's encumbrances, not mine, was inspirational. Getting rid of them was like casting off lead weights, the result sheer joy.

With the New Dawn will come the realization that most of the world's sickness is caused by male leaders dominated by the demands of their egos. In the past, this led to atrocities and tyranny. Current technological advances, coupled with rampant consumerism, could lead to far worse calamities, but with a new understanding we shall leave the old ways behind. Women will come into their own, not as supplanters of men, but as partners. Alongside the wonders of technology, we shall see the far more wondrous results of the power of love.

17

UPLIFTING HOLOGRAM

The Prince of Wales today, 21st January 2008, made his first appearance as a hologram, when his three-dimensional life-size image addressed the World Future Energy Summit in Abu Dhabi. The prince chose to deliver his speech by hologram rather than to attend the summit in person because the flights would have generated up to 20 tons of carbon waste. The hologram left a carbon footprint equivalent to the energy consumed by a light bulb.

It now strikes me that this could be the means by which the business executives I saw communicating with each other from home, when the New Dawn was revealed, will operate. I know nothing of the technology and had assumed the images were on large television screens, but they could equally well have been holograms. Either way, the saving on energy by substituting communication by image for meeting in person, would be enormous. This is another sign of the New Dawn.

18

WORSE   BEFORE   BETTER

All grandparents think the world is a worse place now than when they were young and most of us believe that grandparents have always thought that way. Youth seems boisterous and disrespectful to the old, we argue, because the oldies have forgotten the adventures and the misdemeanours they got up to when they were young.

There is something in this, but it is not the whole story. Until the 18th Century, the daily life of the great majority, those who lived in the country, was unchanged for centuries. For many it remained unchanged until the 20th. Yet the change between the way of life in the childhood of those now in their seventies and eighties and that of contemporary youth is immeasurably incredibly greater. Children of the 19th Century and the first half of the 20th conformed to a pattern of behaviour set by their parents. Meals were at regular times and after sitting at the dining table, children asked for permission to 'get down'. Indoor entertainment was provided, if at all, by a radio, and children got their amusement by playing out of doors. Cinema came as a new kind of entertainment and most children attended a special showing on a Saturday. For most children, their only experience of violence came from watching a gangster film.

There is now no pattern of family meals, except on special occasions. Entertainment is continuously available and the favourite pastime of many boys is participating in computerised games in which the object is to wipe out as many of the opposing side as possible. Playing outside is generally unknown for young children because of the threat presented by violence and by paedophiles. In spite of these undesirable manifestations, the great majority of children are cheerful and healthy minded. There is however a growing tendency for children and teenagers to carry weapons, mostly knives, and for these weapons to be used. Among black male children, especially those without a father or father figure, gang culture is prevalent and gun carrying common. Teenagers of all sections of society indulge in periodic binge drinking sessions until they are unconscious.

At the beginning of the 21st Century it can no longer be argued that the behaviour of the young now is no different from that of fifty years ago. Many older people think that this is a reason for despair. For those living in areas where they dare not go into the streets because of violent gangs, this is understandable. There is however another viewpoint. In a materialistic secular society in which God has been relegated to the religious fringes, an awareness of God will not come until the results of ignoring Him are blatantly obvious and unbearable. The situation had to get worse before it could get better.

It may be an exaggeration to say that the fabric of Western society is in shreds, but it is certainly in tatters. It has clearly become a society of which we cannot be proud. But we can be hopeful. We are on the verge of becoming sick of our sickness. The world is ready for the New Dawn.

19

HERALD AND HEROINE

Men are wonderfully inventive: the pyramids, Rennaissance art, the internal combustion engine, television, the worldwide web............ the list is endless. Looking at the complexity of a sugar beet factory one has to wonder if, without innovative men, we would have discovered sugar. Or should we still know only honey?

But men are not so clever when it comes to making use of what they have invented. Dichlorodiphenyltrichloroethane was synthesized in 1874, during the period of great chemical exploration, but its outstanding property was not discovered until 1939, when a Swiss chemist, Paul Hermann Müller, found that the chemical had remarkable insecticidal properties. By the time the Americans came into the Second World War and were fighting in the Pacific and Southeast Asia, areas noted for endemic malaria, they had realized the potential value of the chemical, by now labelled DDT, against malaria-carrying mosquitoes. The solution to malaria, the American army generals decided, was to spray the ponds and moist habitats where mosquitoes bred, eliminating the mosquito population and thus malaria. DDT was also effective against body lice, another hazard for troops in the tropics, and this problem could be solved by using DDT as a dusting powder on bodies and clothes. DDT seemed to be harmless used in these ways and the long-term effects could be studied later. The army, at war, was in a hurry.

By the end of the Pacific war, the chemical manufacturers who produced DDT had such large stockpiles of the chemical that they put pressure on the U.S. government to allow its release for civilian use, and the Department of Agriculture agreed. The popular press enthused, with headlines about the 'insect bomb' and the prospect of the successful war that could now be waged against insects.

It was not just the popular press that became anti-insect campaigners. A small but influential number of men in the U.S. Department of Agriculture wondered how they could make a name for themselves by devising anti-insect programmes. There were some bizarre outcomes.

During the First World War, a South American ant with a nasty sting had entered America through the port of Mobile, Alabama. Because of its sting it became known as the fire ant and spread gradually to most of the southern states. The fire ant caused few problems and attracted little attention until an enthusiast in the Department of Agriculture decided to promote the virtues of a fire ant eradication programme. Suddenly the fire ant was accorded monster status, a despoiler of agricultural land, a killer of birds, livestock and man. The worst that a fire ant does is to build nests about a foot high that can be a nuisance on the land when operating farm machinery. Its sting is about as painful as a bee's or a wasp's and people avoid provoking the ants. Fire ants were now accused, without any evidence, of attacking the young of ground-nesting birds, and of being dangerous to humans and livestock. A huge eradication programme was planned.

New and more powerful insecticides had been synthesized since the discovery of DDT, and it was decided to use two of the most potent, dieldrin and helptachlor, against the fire ants. The long-term effects of these new insecticides were unknown but in spite of this a million acres were treated in the first year. The results were disastrous. Livestock, poultry and pets were killed. Birds were decimated and species living on the ground suffered 100% mortality. Bobwhite quail, one of the game birds that the fire ant had supposedly affected (figures showed them to be actually on the increase), were in many areas eliminated.

The gypsy moth, because its larvae attack the leaves of the oak and of some other hardwood trees in the spring, was also singled out for eradication, using DDT dissolved in fuel oil. In the height of the madness, the authorities in Nassau County, Long Island, the most densely settled area of New York State except for New York City, decided to use aircraft to spray farms and gardens. In the first air assaults, DDT in the most absorbable form, in fuel oil, was showered down on farm workers and commuters and on children playing out of doors. Birds, fish, crabs and any number of useful insects were killed.

One of the persons outraged by this lunacy was Marjorie Spock, younger sister of the paediatrician Benjamin Spock, renowned for his book, *The Common Sense Book of Baby and Child Care*. Marjorie Spock had bought a house on Long Island with a friend, Polly Richards, who was an invalid needing the purest foods. Marjorie Spock had studied organic farming in Switzerland and was practising organic gardening so that she and her friend could eat healthily. During the summer of 1957, state and federal pest control planes sprayed Long Island gardens and farmland with DDT in fuel oil, on one occasion fourteen times in a single day. Since their land was irrevocably compromised and their livestock contaminated, Spock, Richards and several other Long Island residents decided to sue the federal government.

The case attracted publicity and from the first day of the trial, 10th February 1958, Marjorie Spock wrote a summary of the day's events in court and sent duplicate copies to interested contacts. One of these was a young marine biologist who had written a best-selling book, *The Sea Around Us*, which had enabled her to resign from her job in the Fisheries and Wildlife Service to write full-time. She was now looking for a subject for a new book. Her name was Rachel Carson.

Rachel Carson had had a difficult start in life. Her father Robert, an insurance salesman with a minimal income had sought to solve the family's financial problems by acquiring a sixty four acre plot on Colfax Hill, Springdale, sixteen miles out of Pittsburgh, which he hoped to sell off in lots to newcomers, mostly Polish and Hungarian immigrants. He took out an $11,000 mortgage to acquire the land. The idea never paid off.

With Robert Carson away selling insurance most of the time, his wife Maria was left to cope with the property, run as a smallholding, and their three children, Marian, Robert Junior and Rachel. The clapboard house on the property was basic, without central heating, not an unusual feature in the early 20th Century, but without even the standard facility of indoor plumbing. There were no children on Colfax Hill for Rachel to play with, but she did not miss childhood playmates. She later described herself as a solitary child by choice. One of the reasons may have been that she would have been embarrassed to let others see how poorly they lived.

Rachel was a studious child and shone at school with A's in all subjects. She was especially good at composition, early on winning a magazine prize for a short story. Rachel set her sights on becoming a writer and after school enrolled for a degree in English at the Pennsylvania College for Women in Pittsburgh. There were two events of significance in Rachel's first year. During a thunderstorm, with the wind rattling at the windows, she came across Tennyson's line from *Locksley Hall*:

> For the mighty wind arises, roaring seaward, and I go.

These few words made such an impact on Rachel, who lived 300 miles inland and had never seen the sea, that she sensed that somehow her writing would involve sea subjects. The second event was altogether unexpected and seemed to cancel out the first. Rachel was required to take a science subject during her first year to broaden the syllabus and she chose biology, mainly because the professor was the tall, glamorous Mary Scott Skinker who drove her students hard.

Rachel tackled biology like all her other subjects, with intense interest, and the hard-to-please Skinker was impressed. At the same time, Rachel felt her creative juices drying up and the English course losing its appeal. Her decision was sudden and a bombshell to the college, her mother and even to Mary Skinker. She was changing her major subject from English to biology. Seizing the nettle, Rachel straight away dropped her course on the novel and took up chemistry.

Rachel had a lot of catching up to do in the sciences, but the change unleashed new energies. She played basketball, got in the team as a sub, and had a date to the junior prom. After one heavy snowfall Rachel went moonlight sledging with her friends. Rachel particularly enjoyed the biology class field trips, which she had in an amateur way started on the farm at home with her mother.

Rachel graduated as one of only three students in the college that year who attained their degree magna cum laude, and got a full tuition scholarship to Johns Hopkins University in Baltimore, but the postgraduate highlight was secondment to the prestigious Marine Biological Laboratory at Woods Hole, Massachusetts, at the extreme southwestern end of Cape Cod. Rachel's practical involvement with the sea had at least begun. Rachel's aim was to further her research on the cranial nerves of reptiles that she was to undertake at Johns Hopkins. She and her friend Mary Frye often walked the shore at low tide to explore the marine life of the rock pools and Rachel soon became an expert on seashore fauna.

Rachel intended to stay on at Johns Hopkins to get a doctorate, but destiny had other plans. To survive at all at Johns Hopkins and to pay the fees, Rachel was obliged to take a variety of part-time posts, including that of biology tutor at the Dental School of the University of Maryland. Even so she was awarded her M.A., on the development of the pronephros in catfish, by Johns Hopkins in June 1932. It was the Great Depression and the financial situation at Rachel's home made getting a job more important than finishing her doctorate. Rachel's father's health was deteriorating and he contributed little to the family purse. Rachel's older sister Marian, already twice married and with two children, had developed diabetes and could rarely work. In July, without warning, her father collapsed and died on the back lawn and Rachel suddenly found herself the main family breadwinner.

Rachel desperately needed a job and turned to her ex-tutor and now friend, Mary Skinker, who advised Rachel to take the federal civil service examinations in her zoological fields. Rachel sat the junior parasitologist examination in January 1935 and scored 76.5% and then took the junior wildlife biologist and aquatic biologist exams, at which point Skinker advised Rachel to see Elmer Higgins, division chief at the U.S. Bureau of Fisheries. The timing could not have been better. Higgins was in the middle of producing a series of fifty two seven minute radio programmes on marine life and the two writers he had tried up to then had proved unsatisfactory. Although never having seen any of Rachel's writing, Higgins asked her to try her hand at two programmes. They were lively as well as erudite and were well received, and Rachel was hired to finish the series. Higgins then asked her to write an introduction to marine life for the general public.

Rachel's writing aspirations, for so long dormant, were now thoroughly revived and she began a series of articles for the local newspaper, the *Baltimore Sun*, on various aspects of the marine life of Chesapeake Bay. Her first, for the newspaper's Sunday magazine section, was on the life of a mid-Atlantic fish, the commercially important shad. From the first Rachel's main concern was with the conservation of fish resources. The decline in shad numbers she attributed to over-fishing and the pollution of their waters by industrial and civic effluent.

In July 1936, Elmer Higgins found Rachel a berth in the Fisheries Bureau, assisting the team of scientists studying the Chesapeake Bay fishes. Rachel, 29, was five feet four inches tall, weighed 115 pounds and had curly auburn brown hair. Demure and quiet, she impressed her colleagues with her intelligence, strength of purpose and sound character. Rachel compiled biological and statistical data on the region's fish and wrote departmental reports as well as brochures for the public on fish conservation. The line of Tennyson that had so impressed her as a student was being fulfilled. Seaward she had gone, perhaps not roaring, but inexorably.

Rachel continued to write for magazines and by 1940 had signed a contract for a book, *Under the Sea-Wind*, a description of sea birds and marine creatures combining scientific facts with an attractive, almost poetic, presentation. Published on 1st November 1941, the book had not had time to get off the shelves before the 7th December bombing of Pearl Harbour and sold barely two thousand copies.

By the time Rachel Carson got interested in Marjorie Spock's case against the federal government, she was a successful author. Her book, *The Sea Around Us*, published in 1951, had been at the top of the best-seller list for a record 86 weeks, and in first place for 32 of them. By 1957, Rachel was looking for another subject and, without her yet knowing it, the DDT spraying case was helping to push her in the direction she was to take. Because of the publicity surrounding the Long Island spraying hearing, Rachel undertook to write a three part series on the subject of pesticide use for *The New Yorker*. It was not long before she realized that the problems of pesticide abuse were so widespread and serious that they would form the subject matter of her next book.

Rachel, as a scientist, researched accurately and indefatigably. As a writer, she wrote for the public, clearly and with poetry and passion. She was tireless in pursuit of the evidence against pesticides, although she was going through a time of great strain. Her mother died during the course of the book, and Rachel had the responsibility of looking after her great-nephew Roger because there was no other reliable family member to take on his upbringing. Also, a hard swelling appeared on the left side of her chest. She had had a benign tumour removed from her left breast in 1946. The surgeons could not identify the new swelling's exact nature but recommended immediate radiotherapy.

A more minor worry was the title of the book. Several titles, including *The Control of Nature*, had been considered and rejected. The title Rachel chose for the chapter in the book on the effects of pesticides on birds was *Silent Spring*, and it was her agent Marie Rodell who suggested using it as the title of the book.

Rachel chose an allegorical opening, describing a typical small town in the heart of America which lay in a checkerboard of farms, each with its fields of grain set against hillsides given over to orchards. Even in winter the roadsides were places of beauty, where countless birds came to feed on the berries and on the seed heads of the dried weeds rising above the snow. Into this idyllic countryside there crept a blight, as mysterious maladies swept through the flocks of chickens, and the sheep and cattle sickened and died.

The reader from the beginning could feel the pull of the heartstrings. But after the opening fable, *Silent Spring* is a catalogue of incontrovertible arguments and solid facts. The book was a huge success, being chosen by the Book-of-the-Month Club as its October 1962 selection. Supreme Court Justice William O. Douglas described *Silent Spring* as 'the most revolutionary book since *Uncle Tom's Cabin.*'

There was praise from every unbiased source and, from the pesticide manufacturers, scorn and derision. The Velsicol Chemical Company of Chicago, sole makers of heptachlor and chlordane, claimed that they had actionable rights on the grounds of disparagement of their products and threatened to sue Houghton Mifflin, the book's publishers. Houghton Mifflin responded by pointing out that the author had provided very complete source references for all her material. At President Kennedy's next press conference a reporter referred to a growing concern about the long-term effects of DDT and other pesticides, and enquired if the President had asked the Department of Agriculture to take a closer look at the problem. The President replied, 'Yes, and I know that they already are. I think particularly, of course, since Miss Carson's book, but they are examining the matter.'

The Sea Around Us had made Rachel Carson a best-selling author. *Silent Spring* made her a national heroine. CBS devoted one of its *CBS Reports* to the book and included footage of Rachel speaking from her book-lined study at home. She was calm and authoritative, in contrast to her adversary, Dr Robert White-Stevens, representing the views of the pesticide manufacturers, who was attired in a white lab coat and appeared wild and loud-mouthed.

The outcome over the publicity surrounding the book was the appointment of Senator Abraham Ribicoff (Democrat, Connecticut) to conduct a broad ranging review of environmental hazards by a senatorial committee. One of his first invitations to testify was to Rachel and she willingly accepted.

The demure middle-aged woman in the sage-green suit sitting in front of the Ribicoff committee on 4th June 1963 seemed an unlikely champion of human rights, even less a free spirit who was to change the way we think about the environment. Rachel opened her testimony calmly and in complete control, but there was no mistaking the passion: 'The problem you have chosen to explore is one that must be solved in our time. I feel strongly that a beginning must be made on it now ....'

Later, Senator Ribicoff was to recall that what impressed him about Rachel was that she was a true believer. Her testimony had the ring of truth. She was not speaking on behalf of some vested interest or for her own glorification, but for mankind. What he did not know at the hearing, what even Rachel herself did not know, was that within a year she would be dead. Rachel was riddled with cancer, although it was a coronary attack that carried her off in the end.

There could have been no Rachel Carson story but for the disregard of nature's inviolability by men. The lesson to be learned from this crusade by one committed woman is that putting only men in charge of any field of activity is likely to lead to immoderate and aggressive policies being pursued, often with calamitous results. Had Rachel Carson not spoken out when she did, men would have gone on poisoning the atmosphere and the soil, contaminating the whole diversity of living creatures including humans, with toxic chemicals. Rachel Carson was a heroine. She was also a herald of the New Dawn.

WITH RESPECT TO CHINA

There was a country once that assembled the largest trading fleet the world had ever seen and whose leader, just before it sailed, invited the heads of all the important nations to a great round of celebrations in a specially created city. Absent from the celebrations were Europe's heads of state. England, France, Spain and Portugal were considered too backward in terms of trading and scientific knowledge and too unimportant to invite.

The country was China, its leader was Zhu Di, the occasion was the Chinese New Year 1421, and the venue was Beijing. The heads of state, or their most senior envoys, of all the countries of Asia, Arabia, Africa and India gathered for the inauguration of Zhu Di's pride and joy, the capital's opulent and mysterious walled enclave, the Forbidden City.

A few weeks later, on 5th March 1421, the largest fleet ever assembled set sail from Tanggu (now Tianjin) on the Yellow Sea. The fleet's sea captains, all eunuchs, were intent on exploration and with impressing the lesser nations of the world with the power and might of China, but there was no thought of conquest. China wanted to be recognized as the supreme power, but did not intend to be saddled with an empire of barbarians. She was content with impressing humbler nations with her position as the most civilized country on Earth. She would accept homage and tributes in the form of goods or cash, but had no need of extra lands. Her own were enough. China was the Middle Kingdom, her polite reminder that she was the centre of the universe.

When, seventy or so years later, the countries of Europe started to send out their ocean explorers, their ships were well armed. China had invented gunpowder and used it to make fireworks. It was not until the black powder reached Arabia and the West that its real use became obvious, for blowing up and maiming one's enemies. In 1340, the Earls of Derby and Salisbury found themselves at the battle of Tarifa in Spain, and witnessed what the Arabs' cannon did to the Spanish army. By the time of Crécy, just six years later, the English army was using cannons against the French.

China's great fleet of 1421 carried no guns, but assembled on board was a full complement of interpreters, and representatives of the religions of Buddhism, Islam and Hinduism. The West had already started on the road that led to the future, where authority was measured in terms of the explosive power of armaments. China, the laggard, believed that communication and the exchange of ideas between countries was what mattered. It was the Jesuit missionaries allowed into China by the Ming emperors who, in the 17th Century, wishing to assure their hosts of their helpfulness, showed their potential converts how to make cannons.

When we look at China we should view her with respect. China has always had the power to amaze and still does. Present day China deserves to be understood by the rest of the world if only for one reason, its restraint. No other major nation, let alone the one with the largest population ever known and the biggest peacetime army, has behaved (Tibet excluded) with more self-discipline. Humiliation by foreign powers has been a feature of Chinese history, yet now that China has power it has not used it to get even with countries which have abused it in the past. Russia, by contrast, was responsible for her own humiliation by choosing the dead end road of hardline Communism, and its leaders are now reacting with the classical response of men to loss of face, with threats, bullying and the cynical invasion of those countries on its borders which have chosen freedom.

While Europe was still under the clouds of the Dark Ages, China's sense of being the world's paramount nation was justified. The flowering of China's civilization was way ahead of Europe's, experiencing a golden age of poetry in the T'ang dynasty (618 – 907), still unsurpassed, and the invention of wooden block printing. Under the Sung dynasty, from 960 to 1279, landscape painting reached sublime heights and by the 11th century the Chinese were using moveable type, not to be seen in Europe until Gutenberg's experiments in the 1440's, and printing books in huge numbers. China was also the first country to discover cast iron, canal lock gates, the magnetic compass, porcelain, sternpost rudders, kites, wheelbarrows and paper, as well as printing and gunpowder.

If we define civilization as the establishment of farming, building cities and instituting literacy and consumerism, it arose in the Fertile Crescent, the great arc fanning out in the Middle East with the Tigris and the Euphrates as the main radii. As the forests were cleared for farming, so the light sandy soil land was exposed to the elements and after the Mongol invaders had destroyed the ancient irrigation systems of Iran and Iraq, fertile soil gave way to desert. China fared better. With the rich alluvial soil of the two huge valley systems of the Yangtze and Yellow Rivers and, most years, guaranteed rainfall, China was never, it seemed in her glory years, going to be short of food. Under Mao, as with Russia under Stalin, China reached starvation point. Now that China's population is 1.3 billion, and poor farm workers are fleeing the country for factory wages, food is becoming short again and the resulting high food prices will lead to rationing by income.

The history of China continually provides occurrences for the outsider to marvel at. No other country in the world, having assembled huge trading armadas and dominated the world's trade routes, having sailed the vast realms of the Pacific Ocean, mapped the Indian Ocean, rounded the southern capes of Africa (later named Good Hope) and South America (Cape Horn) and discovered the Americas seventy years before Columbus, would have then banned all sea voyages and introduced the death penalty for disobedience.

Astonishment gives way to incredulity when we learn that China not only banned sea voyages, it forgot them. Where other countries have gloried in the feats of their explorers, China, ashamed at the evidence of their efforts to seek out lesser tribes and far-flung barbarians, tried to bury all traces of her explorations.

It may strike the rest of the world strange that at the height of her seafaring powers China cut herself off from the rest of the world, but it was at least a peacable move. Although China, with her huge fleets and expert navigators, was uniquely placed to expand by colonization she was not intent on empire building. She had made regular sorties northwards to attempt to keep the Mongols in order, and at one stage incorporated Nam Viet within its borders but the local guerrillas in the 16th Century, as in the 1970's, showed the invader it was wise not to trespass there. The main objection the Chinese emperors had to territorial expansion was that it would have entailed the risk of contamination by contact with the barbarians. China wished to be alone.

But, as Greta Garbo found, exoticism invites invasions of privacy, and the outside world would not allow China the luxury of solitude. By a quirk of fate, European countries woke up the idea of ocean exploration soon after China had ended it. Almost exactly seventy years after Zhu Gaozhi, Zhu Di's son and successor, had on the day of his enthronement, 7th September 1424, proclaimed the ban on overseas exploration and contact, the Portuguese were knocking on China's door.

Zhu Gaozhi's demand for complete isolation, while understandable, was unrealistic and unworkable. China's southern coastal peoples, independent and a long way from the northern centres of government, had always been fishermen and, whenever it was profitable, traders. It was not long before Portuguese merchants had set up a base (now Macau) near the mouth of the Pearl River, heralding China's long and ambivalent relationship with persistent and intrusive outsiders.

It may have been inevitable that China should open its doors, however reluctantly, to foreign merchants and even missionaries, but her experiences with outsiders confirmed her worst fears. In the wake of the Portuguese came Spanish traders from the Philippines who forced their way up the Pearl River to Canton and, denied official trading permits, started up illegal trading networks in coastal areas of the surrounding province of Kwantung and nearby Fukien. The Dutch East India Company, after failing to take Macau from the Portuguese, established themselves on the coast of Taiwan (then named by the Portuguese Formosa, 'beautiful').

The British, late arriving in 1637, made up for the delay by the force of their arrival, their squadron of five ships shooting its way into Canton and then cheekily selling off its cargo there. Having had a taste of Western traders, the Chinese emperor was so surprised at the polite and gentle approach of a band of Italian Jesuits when they arrived in 1582 that he made the missionaries welcome. The Jesuits' leader, Matteo Ricci, learned the language, was the first foreigner allowed into the interior of China, and spent the last thirty years of his life as a respected scholar in Peking.

The impression made by the Jesuits on the Chinese court, that not all Westerners were money-grabbing traders, had in the long run the unexpected effect of softening the Chinese antagonism to trading. Since the banned traders would resort to smuggling anyway, the Chinese officials decided that they may as well make trade official and have the imperial treasury benefit from a share in the profits. The port of Canton, way to the south, where the inhabitants had always been less scholarly and more commercially minded, could be safely opened for limited trade. The foreigners would of course have to be kept in their place and be subjected to strict rules. These took the form of the Eight Regulations, the main ones being that no warship or arms were to enter the Pearl River, that the trading ships were not to approach nearer to Canton than Whampoa, thirteen miles downstream, and that all trade and negotiations must be conducted with the monopoly of merchants licensed by the imperial court and known as the Co-Hong. The Co-Hong was under the authority of the Hop-Po, who appointed the monopoly's members and acted on behalf of the emperor in Canton. The Hop-Po received a large subscription from each member of the Co-Hong, rumoured to be £55,000, a vast sum, but necessary since the Hop-Po had to make payments to the Governor of Canton, who in turn had to pass on a sizeable slice of his take to the emperor.

As a reminder to the Western traders that they were there on sufferance, they had no rights whatever. If they had complaints, all they could do was to inform the Co-Hong and hope that somebody listened. The monopoly could and frequently did, when displeased by the foreigner's flaunting of the regulations, halt all trade. But not for long, since it was trade that brought the Co-Hong a return on the capital they had laid out in the first place. The flaunting of the regulations almost always involved one trading item: opium.

Like most events in the early stages of civilization, opium cultivation started in the Fertile Crescent. Sumerian ideograms of about 6000 years ago refer to the opium poppy as the plant of joy, and by the time of the great Egyptian civilization opium had attained an important place in medicine. After expanding into Turkey and Greece, opium growing spread steadily eastwards and Arab traders introduced the opium poppy into China in the 7th Century.

Opium when taken by mouth, unless the taker is habituated, causes nausea and stomach cramps, and oral opium addiction is rare. For centuries opium consumption in China was confined to medicinal usage and as a relaxing treat for a few overworked mandarins, who, if a surviving early recipe is anything to go by, took it in cake form. Any opium growing in China must have been local and on a small scale, since from the 15th Century onwards the Chinese were importing opium, along with other drugs and spices, saffron and wormwood among them, from the Dutch trading post of Malacca on the southwest coast of the Malay Peninsula.

Opium was no more a threat in China than elsewhere until Western penetration of the New World led to the discovery of the pipe of peace of the North American Indians and tobacco. The North American Indian belief that tobacco was a valuable medicine, the need for white settlers to participate in peace pipe ceremonies and, above all, the addictive power of nicotine, all combined to ensure that tobacco addiction spread around the world.

It took hold in England in 1665 and the first two Stuart monarchs, James I and Charles I, roundly condemned the practice. Alexis, the second Romanov Czar, had nicotine deviants tortured and exiled, but the Russians became the keenest of smokers. Murad IV, who came to the throne of the Ottoman empire in 1623 aged eleven, had smokers put to death. It is testimony to the power of nicotine that the ultimate penalty did not deter Ottoman smokers and it was Turkish soldiers on Murad's successful campaign to win back Baghdad who passed on the habit to Persia. Portuguese and Dutch sailors helped to spread the habit to the Far East and by 1644 tobacco smoking was so widespread in China that the emperor Tsung Cheng issued a decree banning the practice.

The ban succeeded better than elsewhere, but only because smoking had introduced the tobacco pipe, and the Chinese were able to switch to smoking a substance not then prohibited, opium. Smoking the drug in a pipe reduced the nauseous symptoms produced by oral consumption and the Chinese took to opium smoking as the rest of the world had to tobacco. In 1729 an imperial decree banned the sale and smoking of opium not because the emperor and his officials believed the ban would succeed, but the severity of the penalties – opium retailers were to be strangled and their accomplices imprisoned and then deported 1000 miles away – ought to at least ensure, they reasoned, that the importing of the drug went through the recognized channels, the Co-Hong in Canton, and that the government got its rake-off.

What the Chinese had surpluses of, and what the Western traders wanted, were tea and silk. The problem was that the Chinese would not trade their silk and tea for European trade goods. They insisted on being paid in silver. The stalemate was resolved by the Portuguese who astutely worked out that there was a handsome profit to be made by buying opium in India, where large scale production had long been organized for medicinal use, and selling it in China. The emperor may have wanted foreign traders to pay in silver, but the populace preferred opium.

The Honourable East India Company, England's trading mafia in India and South East Asia, never missed a marketing opportunity and had no intention of letting the Portuguese cream off the Chinese opium market, especially as they were the landlords of India's opium growing farmers. However, wishing to conform to their Honourable title, the Company ostensibly respected the 1729 ban. They got round it by supplying Portuguese traders with the company's Indian opium in exchange for silver, providing the Company with a continuous supply of the precious metal with which to buy China's tea. It also gave rise to the charge that the Company had perfected the technique of growing opium in India and disowning it in China.

China had in effect been reduced to an if-you-can't-beat-them-join-them policy with regard to opium, not a situation with which the Imperial court could ever be happy. By the beginning of the 19th Century, opium addiction in China had grown alarmingly and the country was faced with an adverse balance of payments as the value of imported opium threatened to overtake the revenues from silk, tea and porcelain sales. The stage was set for the entrance of Lin Tse-Hsu.

Lin, although the second son of a poor teacher, had done brilliantly well at the state examinations in the Confucian classics, open to all Chinese males, and risen to become a provincial governor general. Once installed he had set about ridding his province of the opium trade and, unprecedentedly, had succeeded. So when he offered his services to the emperor, promising to stamp out the trade nationally, the emperor listened, and Lin was granted an unheard-of nineteen personal audiences. In late 1838 Lin was appointed Imperial Commissioner with extraordinarily wide powers and the task of ridding China of the opium menace.

Lin, perspiring in the unaccustomed tropical heat, swept into Canton with all guns blazing. The Co-Hong did not know what had hit them. The Viceroy of Canton, used to a pleasurable and well-oiled existence, dropped down in a faint that lasted an hour. Eight days after his arrival, Lin informed the foreign traders that they were to hand over every ounce of opium they possessed. They were to stake their lives on an undertaking never to traffic again. The Co-Hong were solemnly warned about their over-friendly relations with the Barbarians and told to supervise the handing over of the opium. Any failure would result in executions.

The Barbarians, mostly British merchants, did not take Lin's threats too seriously. They had heard it all before. On the last day allowed, they made the customary token gesture and between them handed over 1037 chests of opium. Lin was incensed. He stepped up the river patrols of armed junks to prevent the Barbarians from getting away, put troops on the streets, withdrew all the merchants' Chinese servants and cut off their food supplies.

The arrival of Captain Charles Elliot R.N. with a motley sea force, including the 18-gun sloop *Larne*, raised the morale of the opium traders, but not for long. Elliot was young and inexperienced and was responsible for the lives of 200 merchants. He proposed that all the opium be handed over and, to quell an outcry and possible rebellion, promised that they would be reimbursed by the British government. It was a promise that quickly ensured compliance since opium stocks were at an all-time high, so much having come in from India that supply had exceeded demand and prices were falling. For the first time in its history opium was a drug on the market.

Lin could scarcely believe his luck. He had been expecting the usual drawn-out succession of offers and counter-offers, with the conclusion only being reached after considerable bloodshed. Now he had been presented with all the opium stocks held by the Barbarians, 20,000 chests, without a shot being fired and at absolutely no cost.

For the first time since the encroachments by Europeans had begun, China had gained the upper hand. But the worst period of Chinese humiliation by foreigners was still to come. The author of China's temporary ascendancy, Lin, was to prove the agent of her greatest humbling. Lin's victory over the foreign opium traders, China's first for two centuries, induced in him a feeling of invincibility and when he received a report that one of a gang of drunken sailors from a British vessel withdrawing down the Pearl River had killed a Chinese villager, he acted immediately, demanding that the murderer be handed over. Elliot had compensated the dead man's family, and tried and punished the man thought responsible, but had been unable to prove a charge of manslaughter and refused to hand him over. Lin, furious at being flouted, ordered his troops to march on Macau, where the merchants had joined their families for the off-trading season. Elliot ordered an evacuation of the families and, deciding that a state of war existed, sent a message home asking for British troops. Lin ordered the citizens of Macau not to supply the British merchant ships with food or water and to shoot any Barbarians who came ashore.

The first shots were fired on 5th September 1839, but the British troops did not arrive until the summer of the following year. It did not take them long to rout the Chinese forces, unused to fighting against well armed and organized soldiery, and hostilities ceased with the humbled Chinese signing the Treaty of Nanking in 1842. This stipulated the ceding of Hong Kong to Britain until 1997, and the granting of trading rights in four new ports: Shanghai, Foochow, Amoy and Ningpo. Lin, having spectacularly lost face, was dismissed to the northwest frontier where he served the emperor more quietly but with just as much devotion. In time, as a reward for pacifying rebel Muslims in Yunnan, he was reinstated to the important position of Grand Guardian to the Heir Apparent. Lin was on his way to suppress the Taiping rebellion in 1850 when he died.

History has labelled the Lin-Elliot conflict the First Opium War, in spite of the actual cause having little to do with opium. The so-called Second Opium War had nothing at all to do with opium, resulting from the arrest of the Chinese crew of the merchant vessel *Arrow* by the Chinese authorities in Canton for harbouring a prominent pirate on the ship. The Chinese force also hauled down the Union Jack. The British Representative in Canton demanded release of the crew, and made much of the allegation of an insult to the British flag. The *Arrow*, not only Chinese crewed but also Chinese owned, had been flying the British flag only under a 12-month port dispensation which had expired the previous month. Despite the British having no case against the Chinese, the general feeling had been growing amongst the American and European traders in south China that the Chinese were getting uppity and needed teaching another lesson. The British called in Admiral Seymour, who brought his fleet upriver, bombarding the Chinese forts on the way. After breaching Canton's defensive wall, a British force captured the city, and despatches were sent to the British government, somewhat tardily, to enquire if war was to be declared.

In Britain, opinions were divided. China was a long way away, the grinding Crimean War had only just been concluded, and by the time the Chinese question was up before parliament, the Indian Mutiny had erupted. But the hawkish Palmerston went to the country on the Chinese issue, was successful at the polls, and duly declared war.

The conflict was one-sided and quickly over, concluding in June 1858 with the Treaty of Tientsin, which granted Western powers what they had long wanted: residential representation in Peking; the opening of more ports to Western trade; the right of foreigners to travel in the interior of China. Opium was not mentioned, although in further negotiations in Shanghai later in the year the British succeeded in halving the duty that the Chinese proposed charging on opium imports. The Chinese refused to ratify the treaty and it required the burning of the emperor's summer palace to persuade them. The final humiliation of the Second Opium War was that China was obliged to accept the two things they least wanted – cheap opium imports and, in a nice irony, Christian missionaries.

Despite opium imports being cheaper than China would have liked, the feared escalation in opium addiction did not materialize. The Victorians, ever seeking respectability, turned against the involvement of their own and other countries in converting foreigners into opium addicts, as they had against slavery, and by the beginning of the 20th Century international agreements were in force to abolish opium trading other than for medicinal purposes. By 1913, the production and consumption of opium in China had virtually ceased. Opium was not to be a serious problem again in China until after 1937, when during the Japanese occupation the invaders opened clinics advertising treatment for a range of common diseases. Those attending the clinics were given a cursory medical examination by an unqualified dispenser, recorded in a register as suffering from one of the diseases on the list, and allowed to buy as much medicine as they liked. The patients were told that they would need to persist with the treatment. There were only two drugs supplied, either morphine or heroin. During World War II the Japanese often behaved with cruelty to those in the countries they occupied, but it was only in China that they coldly and calculatingly set out to degrade the population into addicts.

China may have been impractical in the past, seeking splendid isolation, but her experiences with foreigners made such an aim understandable. China now has done what the rest of the world wanted, opened its doors to trade, and shown that when it comes to business, as the overseas Chinese have been demonstrating for centuries, she needs no tuition. Work was a Chinese ethic long before Christianity or Protestants existed.

The Chinese were also early adepts of wisdom. Confucius (551 – 479 BC) was born poor and became a self-educated man, helped by the love and guidance of his widowed mother. In his maturity, Confucius taught that the key to living is *jen*, which can be translated as virtue or magnanimity. When Confucius was asked its meaning, his most succinct reply was 'Love mankind'.

The Chinese have drifted away from the Confucian ideal, just as the whole world has departed from the teachings of its religious leaders. China's leaders, unelected and almost exclusively men, are not communists but pragmatists who believe that their form of leadership has the great advantage over democracy in that they do not have to bow to public opinion, the voice of their own people. The present Chinese leadership believe that they can with impunity trample down the people of Tibet and imprison and torture their own citizens who are seeking democracy.

The only reason that the Chinese leadership will not allow democracy is that they do not trust the Chinese people. Male oligarchies start off as dictatorial and become increasingly despotic, and China is no exception. Freedom will need to come from the grass roots. China once knew that creating bad karma brings bad consequences, and its leaders will need to relearn this truth. China's hope, as for the rest of the world, is the message of love of the New Dawn.

21

WORSHIP

The traditional religions, saddled with a weight of dogma from the past, are in decline, but that does not prevent individuals from still being strengthened by their faiths, as anyone who has attended a Christian church on Sunday, a synagogue on the Sabbath, or a mosque on Friday will have witnessed. The Eastern religions are not restricted to such formal patterns of worship. When I was visiting the Observatory on its mound in Jaipur, I happened to look down to see a simple circular temple in the street below. Round its domed roof were stood to dry a ring of cow dung patties that are the fuel of the poor in India. While I was taking in the rightness of this useful practice, an Indian man on an ancient bicycle drew up at the temple door. He went inside and reappeared five minutes later, mounted his bike and rode off. There was something wonderfully refreshing about this spontaneous act, illustrating how religion is interwoven in the daily life of Hindus rather than set aside for a special day of worship.

Since I have had harsh words to say about the dogmatic aspects of the Western religions, I have been aware that some acknowledgement of the value to society of the faithful worshipper was required, but I did not know how to express it.

As throughout this book, when I have needed help it has come. This time it is in the shape of my bedtime reading, which at the moment is the absorbing biography of Hilaire Belloc by A.N. Wilson. Belloc was a rumbustious eccentric who, being born in France, was a republican and a Catholic, yet he chose to live in England. Despite his criticism of the monarchy and most other British traditions, Belloc was a gifted writer, an outstanding companion and masterly conversationalist, and endeared himself to many of the great and the good of the Edwardian era. His many drinking friends included Maurice Baring and G.K. Chesterton, and he was a friend of Shaw and Wells.

In the summer of 1901 Belloc decided on impulse to walk from Toul in northern France (he had done his national service there) to Rome and write a book, not so much about the places en route as about his impressions. It was not a pilgrimage. Belloc's Catholic faith, although often brandished, had faded. The book was called *The Path to Rome* and included an account of Belloc's pause in the Alpine village of Undervelier where, smoking a cigar, he watched the entire population of the village stream into the church for Vespers. Belloc put down his cigar, saving it under the capping stone of a wall, and followed the villagers into the church. Inside, his vision of the Catholic Church and of its history and place in the world was renewed. After the service Belloc came out, retrieved his cigar and, stirred by his experience in the church, continued his deep reverie, moved to tears.

Belloc continued on his journey, his faith renewed, and not all the atheistic cynicism in the world can deny that he was not the better for it. The solidarity of the village faith of Undervelier is of an age that has passed, but we need not grieve. The freedom and joy discovered by the children of the New Dawn will signal the rebirth of hope in our hearts and our rediscovery of God.

22

THE ULTIMATE PARTICLE

Some time during this summer of 2008 will be conducted a scientific experiment that will be the longest awaited ever and perhaps the most momentous. In a 16¾ mile tunnel built by CERN, the European Organization for Nuclear Reserach, under the Jura mountains in Switzerland, has been assembled the most complex machine ever built. The machine is designed to accelerate subatomic particles and is known as the Large Hadron Collider. It will not split atoms but perform the far more difficult feat of splitting protons.

All scientific experiments are designed to test in one way or another the validity of a theory and in this instance the CERN scientists are seeking to find out if the theory put forward by physicist Peter Higgs in 1964 is tenable. What Higgs was trying to solve was a most fundamental unsolved question in particle physics: what holds subatomic particles together? If we take the familiar analogy of an atom the size of the Albert Hall, then almost all of it is space, with a nucleus the size of a pea at the centre and an electromagnetic particle the size of a speck of dust whizzing round the periphery. The mystery is that, since gravity is far too weak a force, no one knows what holds the particles together and Higgs proposed that it might be done by a field of ethereal glue, the Higgs field. Other physicists have postulated that the field might be composed of ultra-tiny particles which they called Higgs bosons.

The apparatus for the experiment consists of a waist-high tube fitted with hugely powerful electromagnets and during the experiment atoms are split and the resulting protons harvested into a fine thread and directed around the tube at ever increasing speed by the electromagnets. One thread of protons is sent one way round the tube and another thread in the opposite direction and the two threads collide at nearly the speed of light at a point in the tube monitored by a 'camera' the size of an office block and called the Atlas detector. The Atlas detector records the particles resulting from the collision of protons and it is hoped that it might catch sight of a Higgs boson or two.

Needless to say the experiment is not as simple as that. Other CERN physicists hope that the proton collision, simulating conditions in the universe a millisecond after the Big Bang 13 million years ago, will explain why at that time all matter was not wiped out by anti-matter, a consequence which the currently accepted Standard Model of the cosmos says should have occurred, in which case there would be no universe or humans in it to worry about such matters.

The main objective of physics at present is to find a theory that unifies the laws relating to the large dimensions, represented by gravity and general relativity, with those relating to the very small, as represented by quantum theory. The result will be a 'theory of everything' called quantum gravity. In the 1990's Professor Stephen Hawking believed that the odds of finding the unified theory by the end of the millennium were 50/50. New discoveries and, perhaps more to the point, new theorizing, have led Professor Hawking to predicting that finding the theory may take a little longer. He is sure that we shall find our universe to be one of many. One of his many distinctive sayings is 'Our universe is like a crazy dance of waves, tangoing to a myriad beats', relating to the fact that, even in a vacuum, a pair of particles can pop into being out of nowhere.

Physicists right now are not sure whether there are 10 or 11 dimensions of time, although some say 27. The number of universes? No one knows. Professor Itshak Bars of the University of Southern California envisages the passage of time as curves embedded in six dimensions, four of space and two of time.

There is a very slight possibility that the CERN experiment will cause a chain reaction more powerful than any man-made nuclear explosion, but physicists judge the likelihood of this to be remote. Martin Rees, the Astronomer Royal, puts the chance of it happening as one in 50 million. The total cost of CERN so far is $8 billion and Britain's annual contribution is £73 million. The size of the carbon footprint created by the experiment has not been disclosed but is likely to be elephantine.

The CERN experiment is of interest because it exemplifies a characteristic of males. A few women physicists work for CERN but it is, like all cutting edge science, essentially run by men. A tiny proportion of males feels a strong urge to want to explore what has not been explored before regardless of cost or consequences. The rest of us admired the conquest of Everest, were awed by the landing on the Moon and are meant to be agog about the results of the imminent super-collision of protons in the CERN tunnel, but should we, the taxpayers of Europe who are paying for the experiment, be enthusiastic? The answer must be no.

The first objection is that were the taxpayers given a chance to vote on the expenditure they would almost certainly vote against it. The allocation of CERN funds, like so much else, is taken by governments without any consideration of the views of the electorate. Such decisions are basically undemocratic. With so much poverty in the world, the $8 billion CERN money could have been spent more wisely and humanely.

Although I shall be very interested in the CERN results, I would have been happier to see the money better spent. There is another reason that I doubt the value of the CERN experiment. I believe the Standard Model to be inherently flawed. There appears to be an assumption by physicists of an ultimate miniscule particle smaller than which it is not possible to go. Yet if the universe is outwardly infinite, it must be infinite in the direction of subatomic particles. If there is an infinity viewed through the telescope, there must be an infinity viewed through the microscope.

I believe that the forthcoming CERN experiment will fail to provide final answers to physicists' uncertainties about matter and the smallest subatomic particles, for the reason that the current Standard Model paradigm is flawed by not taking into account the infinity of particles of subatomic size. Even if the results of the CERN experiment point in that direction, it will be small consolation for the profligate expenditure. This is written on 27th February 2008. The writer was awarded a matriculation credit in physics, equivalent to today's 'O' level, in 1943.

23

KULA MEN, WARMER WOMEN

The CERN experiment exemplifies the irrepressible desire of mankind – meaning men - to push the boundaries of knowledge beyond present limits. At least that is how we like to think of such endeavours, and we have been able to take such a rosy view so far for one main reason. Such expansion of knowledge came free. Newton worked out gravity with a quill pen and some parchment. Einstein formulated relativity using a fountain pen and a few sheets of foolscap.

But the pursuit of knowledge can no longer be accomplished in the minds of geniuses. Now, expensive technology is required and, almost always, costly computers to process the results. The CERN experiment requires a building the size of a small hotel to house the thousands of computers needed to process the information fed to it from the collision detector. The CERN experiment, and others such as the Star Wars antimissile programme being pursued by the United States, are only just affordable now. With the global economy on the downturn, profligate technological spending on this scale may have to give way to what is affordable. Food rather than arms or technology is likely to become the priority in the immediate future.

Soon we shall need to face the fact that our benign view of the frontiers of knowledge being heroically pushed back to the sound of trumpets consists mostly of our witnessing the working out of the obsessive-compulsive disorders of a small proportion of men. During the 2 million years of mankind's hunter-gatherer era, the human race had enough to do to survive. Once farming came into the picture and, crucially, farming surpluses that could be traded, we took the quick route to cities and civilization.

Suddenly, fifteen to twenty thousand years ago, as if to compensate for the endless millennia when nothing much had happened, there appeared big countries and vast empires, great cities bursting at the seams. The facilitators for the advance were armies. The size of the hunter-gatherer groups was limited to how many wives the alpha male could defend and the number of younger males he could control. Once a leader could pay the wages of an army, the size of his fiefdom was incomparably enlarged. How far the leader could enlarge his army and his territory depended on the skill of the leader, the quality of his troops, which relied on the nature of the people he was recruiting from, and good or bad fortune. His subjects took what came. At least most of them did. The leader always needed an entourage to stay at home and run things and, especially, to keep the revenue flowing. The leader, by his conquests, determined how large the empire would become, but it was the stay-at-home men who shaped the ethos of society. The fact that the first large functional buildings to have been discovered, those in Uruk in southern Mesopotamia, from the 4th millennium B.C. Sumerian civilisation, were temples, make it clear that priests ruled the roost from the beginning of civilization.

There were plenty of sensible men and women around but it was the obsessive-compulsive men driven to invent some belief, whether it was in a bird god who demanded that their priests dress in feathers or a bull god who required the living hearts torn out of sacrificial victims, who took the lead and ran things. Ludicrous their beliefs may have been, but strong beliefs displace less fervently held ones, however reasonable, and hold sway until a stronger belief comes along.

Hunter-gatherer men were occupied with survival, had no time or inclination to invent fancy religions, and appreciated the contribution of women. Once civilisation came, men seemed to need to balance the material advantages by inventing weird belief systems to hold society together. Women, without an inbuilt need to invent bizarre belief edifices, had no hope of taking the lead, or of even having appreciable influence, once the civilization process got under way.

It will help to understand the deep seated need of men to invent belief systems if we look at the Kula. Kula is a unique ritual of exchange participated in by men of the Trobriand Island group that was studied and then recorded by the renowned ethnologist Bronislaw Malinowski in his 1922 classic, *Argonauts of the Western Pacific*. The Trobriand Islands lie off the eastern tip of Papua New Guinea, distributed in an irregular circle roughly a hundred miles across, and the two items that were circulated and exchanged in the ritual were necklaces of red shell, called *soulava*, and arm bracelets of white shell called *mwali*. An elite band of men in each village took part in the Kula. Prospective Kula participants were selected as boys and trained in the formalities, spells and secret arts.

Those carrying a *soulava* necklace set off in a clockwise direction round the islands and those bearing a *mwali* armband in an anticlockwise circuit. At each appointed meeting place the *soulava* carrier handed over a necklace to his opposite number, a *mwali* carrier, who would hand over in exchange an armband. The Kula exchange was usually accompanied by an elaborate ceremonial and the necklaces and armbands were treated with almost religious reverence. Those taking part in an exchange became Kula partners for life. The recipient would keep the armband or necklace for a limited period, usually a few months, and then it would be passed on in a subsequent Kula exchange further along the island circuit. A Kula participant would be away from home for anything up to 18 months. Some trading might be carried out during the Kula voyage, but its purpose was the ritual exchange of necklaces and armbands.

Nobody knows when the Kula was started, but we can be fairly sure why. Trobriand Island men could no longer bear the simple life growing yam, taro and sugar cane, of fishing and canoe building. They needed a purpose, a justification for living.

Inventing the Kula gave to the men a meaning to all aspects of life. Canoe building was no longer a routine necessity but part of the Kula ritual. The Trobrianders, like all Pacific islanders, had always built canoes, but with the advent of Kula, canoe building took on a magical and almost religious significance. Magic rites had to be employed to prepare the canoe for the Kula journey, starting with the selection of a suitable tree to provide the trunk to be shaped into the canoe hull. Once the tree had been chosen, its tree spirit needed to be propitiated and this was done by making a small incision in the trunk into which a piece of areca nut or some other titbit was inserted. A whole series of rites and spells continued during the building of the Kula canoe. Then came the whole business of the sacred circular tour.

It may seem to those of us without a Kula involvement that to select shell necklaces and armbands of no intrinsic value for ritual exchange was somewhat bizarre, that to specify that necklaces must travel clockwise and armbands anticlockwise was arbitrary in the extreme, that for males to absent themselves from home and family and from tending the garden for up to 18 months was selfish and unfair to their partners. But the Kula was an invention of sanity and light compared with what most groups of men in most places have, since the hunter-gatherer era, dreamt up as a justification for living.

On a much larger island than any in the Trobriand group, in the South China Sea, a different and less benign form of the male rationale for living was invented a few hundred years ago. On the island of Borneo it had long been the tradition among the Sea Dyak tribes, more correctly known as Iban, and by the Kayan and Kenyah peoples, for the men to take home to the longhouse, as a trophy, the hair of those they had killed in battle. No one knows why they changed to taking whole heads as trophies, although according to the classic Kenyah folk tale on the subject, the revered Rajah Tokong, on a raiding party, was advised to take up the practice by a frog. Why only take the hair, the frog asked the Rajah, which is of such little use, when by taking the whole head he would gain everything he required, a good harvest, freedom from sickness and good fortune.

During the next attack on a rival longhouse, Tokong's party took a number of heads and brought them back home in a basket. They found that they could travel more quickly and without fatigue, that once they were in their boats the river current bore them speedily home, and that not only had the rice grown knee-deep while they were away, but that their families at home were all thriving and in the best of health and the lame now walking.

Well, it is a better story than the reality, which is that men thought up head-hunting to give a meaning to life. The significant development in Bornean head-hunting was that from originally being symbolic, a trophy record of a particular raid, head-hunting became, in true

Kula fashion, an end in itself. It was heads hanging up in a longhouse that gave the inhabitants good harvests and good fortune, and raiding parties went out with the sole purpose of bringing home heads.

James Brooke, the first White Rajah of Sarawak, started to put down the practice in the 19th Century and during the reign of his successor, his nephew Charles Brooke, head-hunting was eliminated. But it was not forgetten. In an Iban longhouse far up the Rejang river in the late-1950's an elderly widow showed me with considerable pride the thirty three knots of hair tied to the handle of her late husband's *parang*, the machete of Borneo and Indonesia. The taker of heads retained the hair as a trophy and the shaven heads were kept in a ceremonial basket above the communal fire, gradually turning into blackened skulls. Men it was who had thought up head-hunting as a *raison d'être*, but, as with Kula, once it became invested with religious significance, the whole community adopted it as their creed.

Head-hunting in Borneo has ended but, perhaps surprisingly, the Kula goes on in the Trobriand Islands. Kula journeys are still mostly taken in the ceremonial canoes, although such is the importance of the Kula even now that occasionally motor boats and aeroplanes are used. There has been a shift of emphasis. Before, the Kula was paramount and the trading aspect insignificant. Now, those Kula members who have owned high-ranking shells, those armbands or necklaces that have been in circulation the longest, have such a high standing in their communities that they are usually prominent in business. Kula has taken a step in the direction of one of those other inventions of men looking for a purpose in life, Freemasonry.

The results of the Kula tendency in men have ranged from the merely amusing to the obscenely cruel. By the 15th Century, the Aztecs in Mexico had refined their religious rituals to a point where human sacrifice was not only the key act of worship but so highly thought of that volunteers, mostly young girls, offered themselves as sacrificial victims, thus gaining for themselves a happy eternal life. In the American Museum of Natural History there is a graphic depiction of a sacrificial victim being held down by priests while another rips out the beating heart. There was a special celebration every 52 years on the Huixachtécatl mountaintop when the priests lit a fire on the breast of a victim.

The Roman Catholic officers of the Inquisition also favoured fire as means of execution of heretics since it showed that the Church was avoiding actual bloodshed. The Inquisitors justified their activities on the basis that God had been the first Inquisitor when he had expelled Adam and Eve from the Garden of Eden, and that excommunication, the severest penalty until then, had proved an insufficient deterrent to those heretics deviating from the Church dogma of the time. Occasionally errors were made. Joan of Arc was mistaken for a witch and burned at the stake in Rouen in 1431, only to be rehabilitated four years later and eventually canonised.

Although there were instances of the burning of heretics before the 13th Century, the Inquisition proper got its impetus from the Fourth Lateran Council, opened by Pope Innocent III in November 1215. By the 15th Century, the Inquisition was well under way. It had thus taken 1400 years for the message of love and forgiveness of the founder to be translated into burnings at the stake for perceived non-compliance with Church dogma. It is interesting that it has taken a similar time for a belief in Allah the Merciful to be now interpreted as requiring some followers to kill themselves along with as many unbelievers as possible.

In case we think that men's Kula propensities were a feature of the past or confined to faraway places, we need look only at Scientology, founded in 1952 by science fiction writer, L. Ron Hubbard. Scientology is a new religion catering to those individuals, mostly men, who cannot find any alternative justification for living. Its central belief is that 75 million years ago, 13.5 trillion aliens were banished to Earth by a warlord called Xenu. As if that were not bad enough, the exiled aliens were dropped into volcanoes and vaporised with nuclear bombs. The souls of these unfortunates, known to Scientologists as thetans, then latched on to humans and are believed the cause of most human problems, both individual and social. The only remedy for the thetan-damaged soul is to take part in 'audits' with a trained Scientology counsellor. The audited Scientologist then has the opportunity to rise though the movement to ever increasing levels of seniority.

Scientology has from its inception been strong in California and popular with some famous Hollywood film stars, including John Travolta and Tom Cruise. It is a testimony to the strength of the Kula phenomenon that otherwise rational human beings can be taken in by such sci-fi absurdity. Scientology leads one to recall Dr Johnson's remark about the dog walking on its hind legs, the surprise being not that it is not done well, but that it is done at all. The atheist and ultra-rational Professor Richard Dawkins describes Scientology, in his *The God Delusion*, as the 'one religion that was intelligently designed, almost in its entirety'.

Today there is much right with the world. We in the West, even if not yet everywhere, have learned that democracy offers the best promise of citizens living a fulfilled life. We have learned that the free market economy has the potential to rid us of poverty. What we have not learned, because men are still running almost all that matters, is moderation.

Men have tunnel vision. Whether they settle on human sacrifice, the Inquisition, head-hunting or market forces, they pursue their goal to the ultimate, until the consequences become unbearable. The current male obsession is the free market. For a century and a half the obsession for a sizeable proportion of the world's males was the bleak doctrine of Marxism, and when that had been tried and shown to fail, the free market became men's idol. The concept that the creation of wealth can be left to the unrestrained competitive individual may work in the short term and for a time even benefit the majority of individuals in a society. But it will never be of benefit to society as a whole because the creation of wealth is not what we are here for. We are here, each one of us, to explore the possibilities of applying love in whatever situation we find ourselves.

There was a time, not so long ago, when banks were the trusted guardians of the fiscal economy. Cautious, ponderous even, their policy was one of safe and sound investment with the minimum of risk. Because there are now fortunes to be made in allocating vast amounts of capital to bet – banks use the word hedging - on currency fluctuations and in wagering on the rise or fall of stock market indices, banks entrust billions to young men to play the markets. As this is being written, news is being released of a young Frenchman who has lost his bank £3.7bn through unauthorised, that is to say unsupervised, futures trading. He managed to place more than £50bn in unauthorised futures trades before the losses were discovered. The bank, Société Générale, is unlikely to survive. If any lesson were needed from this, it is that greed is not a sound basis for banking.

The destabilisation of banking is just one of the current symptoms of the world sickness that is the result of allowing men to run everything of importance. The doctrine of free market forces that became the latest male Kula belief towards the end of the last century started off as a liberating business philosophy. It is now being used as a justification for corporate greed on a massive scale. Jeff Randall, financial journalist and high priest of the free market philosophy, recently described the current debt-laden way of living in the West as the economics of the madhouse.

In 1980 the daily average of foreign exchange trading totalled $80bn. Today it is probably over $2000bn. When the banks and finance houses discovered that gambling in international money markets and in futures trading produced more profits than financing the production of merchandise and services, they took the easier but riskier route. The annual global trade in goods and services is now merely the equivalent of a day or two's trading on the foreign exchange markets. Unfettered economic growth has not only pushed pollution and global warming levels to dangerous levels, but it has failed to help the poor. Twice as many people on the planet live in absolute poverty as in 1950.

In less than 20,000 years man has progressed from an illiterate innocent, a slightly superior ape, to a greedy super-technologist who is in danger of turning the environment of the planet into a wasteland incapable of sustaining the species in its present way of life. Many individuals have accumulated wealth beyond imagining, yet millions of the poor starve to death. What has gone wrong?

Round about two million years ago, when man took the first steps to becoming human rather than an advanced ape, the brain responded by developing larger left and right cerebral hemispheres. Communication between the two hemispheres is by means of the corpus callosum, a mass of nerve tissue the shape of an inverted saucer. Research has shown that in more recent times, the need to process language, the written word and technology has resulted in increased traffic between the two hemispheres and that the corpus callosum has found it hard to handle the extra load. As a result, each cerebral hemisphere, experiencing delays in transmitting to its partner, has gradually specialised in its own tasks.

This specialisation has resulted in the left hemisphere containing a higher concentration of brain cell nuclei, the grey matter, than the right. The shorter connections make for quicker contacts between the cells and fit the left brain for high-speed smart tasks such as language and mathematical processing, what might be called areas of expertise. The less crowded right brain, having longer connections between the cells, is better suited to less speedy but more complex functions correlating activity from different brain regions. The consensus approach of the right brain gives it a more intuitive, holistic approach and the caring professions have a high proportion of those with highly developed right brains.

Anatomists specialising in measuring human brains find that about half the population have a larger than average corpus callosum, allowing better communication between the two halves of the brain. Studies by psychologists have shown that the 50% of individuals with a well endowed corpus callosum are especially good at communicating, multi-tasking and expressing their emotions. In other words, at being more caring individuals. The half of humanity having these benefits are characterised by another feature. They are women.

The world's problems may now be seen in a different light. By allowing men to run the world we have been rewarded with any number of smart answers to difficult questions because men ask: How can we find an answer to this problem? How can we fix this to make it work better? What women ask and men do not is: How will this solution affect people? Will it be of help?

By denying women a say in the major decision making of the world, we have ignored the effect on people of industrial and technological progress, of free market globalisation. The answer to many of the world's problems is not to get women to take over from men, but to at least allow them to have as much say as men. Then we shall see women make the huge contribution to business and public life that has been denied them for so long. The human race, as well as being clever, will, in the New Dawn, become caring. We will even dare to use and promote the concept and the word that is not included in the daytime vocabulary of most males: love.

24

HEALTH MATTERS BUT NOT TOO MUCH

Yesterday was Chinese New Year and there was a double cause for celebration because I had finished the book. I felt like gathering up the sackful of newspaper cuttings and the hundreds of notes written on the back of old A4 sheets, piling them in the garden and having a celebratory bonfire. The thought of the resulting carbon pollution stopped me, and after enjoying in my mind an imaginary and symbolic bonfire I put the papers in the recycling bin.

During the night my celebratory sleep was interrupted. The book was not finished, the voice said. I had not written about health and healing.

It was clear from the beginning that I was not in charge of this book and since the Lecturer departed it has been a tentative business, with my having to rely on jogs and nudges from a more gentle and less authoritative mentor. There was only one thing I had been sure of. There was to be nothing on medical matters. I had been immersed in the world of medicine since I was sixteen. Even when I retired from pharmacy I ended up writing about health and medicine. With this book, all that was behind me. I was now on a higher plane.

But I no longer argue with the voice. I shall start at the beginning and see what comes. At least it is a subject I know something about.

I was nearly sixteen and, having taken the school certificate examinations, I was leaving the Wyggeston School, Leicester in three weeks. I had no idea what I was going to do. I wanted to study medicine but this was before the 1948 Education Act and university grants, and there was no possibility of my widowed mother supporting me for two years in the sixth form and then for six years as a medical student. With the exams over, we were mostly left to our own devices but on this particular day there was a period scheduled for going over the English Literature paper. When I went into 5 Science form room, those who were leaving were talking about the jobs their fathers had lined up for them. The Wyggeston was Leicester's top school, mainly for fee-paying pupils and I was one of the minority of scholarship boys. Envious at the smugness around me, and suddenly irked, I blurted out, ' It's all right for you lot! I've no idea what I'm going to do.'

Raymond Bowler, my fellow chemistry fanatic at the other side of the room, looked across owlishly through the circular lenses of his glasses and said, 'You want to go in for pharmacy. My brother did and he's earning ten pounds a week.' I had been brought up as a Primitive Methodist and knew all about God looking after sparrows (Matthew10.29) but it was many decades later that I realized He looks after people too.

It was an exciting time to be entering any branch of medicine. A week after starting my pharmacy apprenticeship, an article in *The Times* drew attention to a remarkable therapeutic substance, under the headline 'Penicillium'. I already knew about the sulphonamides. My Aunt Dora, one of my two nursing aunts, had come home one weekend bursting with the news about *M & B 693*, sulphapyridine, the new drug that was effective against pneumonia. She did not mention the fact, but I realized that if it had been available a few years earlier it would have saved my father. Double pneumonia, pneumonia in both lungs, had killed him at the age of 33.

It was writing up the penicillin story for the *Pharmaceutical Journal* many years later that led me to take an interest in and to write about the history of medicine. Until then I had held the standard view of slow but steady progress and then the discovery of the first antibacterial drugs, the sulphonamides and penicillin, and then from the middle of the 20th Century the flood of new drugs effective for all manner of conditions, a pill for every ill.

The surprise was finding that for over 1600 years there had been virtually no progress in medicine at all, that in fact the medicine practised throughout that time was harmful rather than beneficial. Hippocrates founded what might be called modern medicine by taking two big steps forward. He separated medicine from religion, and he differentiated between different diseases. Previously healing had been temple-based, under the auspices of Aesculapius the god of healing, and all sickness had been regarded as one great disease.

Hippocrates, born somewhere around 460 BC on the island of Cos, lived at the time of the great flowering of the Greek intellect, in the age of Pericles and a short time before Plato and Aristotle. His place of honour as the father of medicine is deserved if only because he introduced diagnosis, distinguishing between the young man with a gaunt frame, hollow cheeks and a racking cough and the patient with a high fever, pain in the chest, an intermittent cough and delirium. Although he did not label them with the later names, he was distinguishing between tuberculosis and pneumonia.

Hippocrates preached that healing requires study of the facts, that facts are only obtained by close examination and that deductions are based on observations, not according to the phase of the Moon or from consulting a temple oracle. The descriptions that Hippocrates left, based on keen and careful observation, remain models of their kind. Hippocrates was a modest man, aware of the paucity of medical knowledge of the time and, more importantly, that the ill body has a strong tendency to get better. Hippocrates knew that it was often enough to simply help the body recover, to stimulate what the Romans were to call the *vis medicatrix naturae*, the body's own defence mechanism, and he advised restraint in treatment. W.H. Auden's ideal doctor was an endomorph with gentle hands, and one can't help thinking that Hippocrates would have fitted the bill.

The next individual to influence medicine was a very different character. Galen was born in 129 in Pergamum (now Bergama, Turkey), the son of a gifted architect who had the money to send his ambitious son for medical training in Smyrna, Corinth and Alexandria. Returning to Pergamum, Galen got himself appointed as a physician to the gladiators there and had plenty of opportunities to study wounds and to try out treatments. But patching up gladiators in the provinces quickly palled, and the young and thrusting Galen was soon in Rome, flattering the rich and powerful and moving up the medical ladder.

Galen's ascent was inexorable and, for medicine, fatal. Hippocrates had been a gentleman and a gentle man. Galen was a braggart and a showman and soon after his arrival in Rome we find him before a large crowd in the forum. He has slit the throat of a pig to make it squeal and, having secured the crowd's attention, he makes a few flourishes with a scalpel in hand and severs the laryngeal nerves, producing a sudden dramatic silence, soon broken by the applause of the crowd.

When the emperor, Marcus Aurelius, felt under the weather on one occasion and was dissatisfied with the diagnosis of his doctors, he sent for Galen to give a second opinion. The doctors had predicted that the emperor was about to go down with a full-blown fever. Galen, knowing Roman eating habits and the emperor's appetite, calmly announced that the great man merely had indigestion. Marcus Aurelius almost immediately perked up, and Galen's reputation was made.

Galen, with the egotist's insatiable appetite for praise and wanting to secure a place in the medical pantheon, wrote incessantly. His treatments were as ineffectual as those of any other doctor at the time – his favourite remedy was a concoction of seventy two ingredients including vipers' flesh and ground-up lizard – but the sheer volume of his writings impressed the profession. Without adding a jot to medical knowledge, he wrote sixteen volumes on the pulse.

Galen backed the humoral theory of medicine held at the time, based on the completely unfounded notion that the health of the body depended on the correct balance of the four humours, blood, phlegm, yellow bile and black bile. With Galen's endorsement, this remained the accepted basis of medicine for another 1600 years. That would have been bad enough, but Galen left a more ruinous legacy. Hippocrates had advocated mild purging and bleeding for some conditions. Such restraint failed to satisfy Galen's inflated ego and he introduced drastic purging and copious bleeding. Both procedures weakened ill patients, bleeding sometimes fatally so. Most excessive bleeding treatments that resulted in the demise of patients went unnoticed. The physician naturally attributed death to the disease and not the treatment. One case was, however, well documented.

George Washington was unlucky, happening to fall ill late in life when heroic medicine in America was at its drastic peak, largely due to the influence of one man. Benjamin Rush, born in Philadelphia in 1745, was a charismatic figure who blazed trails in several fields. A signatory of the Declaration of Independence, he campaigned zealously for national universities, the education of women and the abolition of slavery. Sound on most issues, he was only blindly dogmatic when it came to medicine, which unfortunately was his chosen career. After graduating from Princeton University at the age of 15, Rush studied medicine in Edinburgh, absorbed its modestly heroic principles but decided that there was no point in being half-hearted about treatment. Returning to America in his late 20's, Rush became professor of medicine at Philadelphia University and was soon announcing his intentions by assuring his students that it was 'a hard matter to bleed a patient to death'. Another Galen had arrived.

Normally such reckless advice would have affected only a minority of students, but Rush's influence on the medical scene in America was unparalleled. Philadelphia was one of four medical schools in the country at that time, but during the 44 years of Rush's tenure there, it produced three quarters of all doctors who qualified, all indoctrinated with the belief that purging and bleeding were the paramount treatments.

Rush elevated bleeding to new and lethal heights, his recommendation for pneumonia being the drawing of 140 fluid ounces (4 litres) of blood during the treatment period, an amount not far short of the total blood volume. That not all his patients died was due to the remarkable ability of the body to manufacture replacement blood cells. Rush employed huge doses of calomel, mercurous chloride, as a purgative and when copious salivation and other symptoms of mercury poisoning resulted, he welcomed them as signs of 'mercurial fever', which he believed was a prelude to recovery. When the patient died, as frequently happened, the death was attributed to the original disease.

Fatefully for George Washington, he began to feel unwell in the early hours of Friday 13th December 1799 with a sore throat, probably resulting from a thorough soaking the day before. He developed a fever and when his breathing became laboured, Washington thought that he needed treatment and, so imbued was the idea of bleeding as a cure-all, that he sent for a local bleeder who drew a pint or so of blood from his arm. Washington slept fitfully, and being no better in the morning he sent for his personal physician, Dr James Craik, who arrived at 11 a.m. Seeing the seriousness of the patient's condition, Craik sent for two of his colleagues and pending their arrival he busied himself with the obligatory heroic procedures, carrying out two more copious bleedings, and administering two purging doses of calomel and a purging enema. All these measures, as the report on Washington's death put it, were 'to no avail'.

The colleagues Craik called in were Dr John Brown and Dr Elisha Dick, and when they arrived, Craik told them that he favoured another blood-letting. Brown supported him but Dick, more sensible and humane, opposed the idea, pointing out that three pints of blood had already been taken from a seriously ill patient. 'He needs all his strength,' Dick cautioned,' and bleeding will diminish it.' But Dick was the junior of the three and was overruled. A further pint and a half was drawn off, although the senior pro-bleeding doctors were later to admit that the procedure was 'without the smallest apparent alleviation of the disease.'

Washington, now suffering from a serious loss of blood as well as from the infection, might have benefited from a quiet regimen of rest and the administration of light nutrient foods, but heroic medicine demanded action and so the tortures went on. The patient was given a dose of 10 grains (0.6g) of calomel that would have been a testing dose for a fit man, and several doses of tartar emetic, a nauseous antimony compound and mild poison, in spite of the fact that there can have been nothing left in the stomach to vomit. Washington had already been subjected to blistering of the throat. This was another heroic medical procedure, when a drastic irritant was applied to the skin to create a blister, the rationale being that as the blister swelled it drew off harmful elements from within. A vinegar poultice was now applied on top of the throat blister, and blistering agents were strapped to the soles of the patient's feet. Washington tried several times to speak through the encumbrances at his throat, and when eventually he could make himself heard, the message was clear. He wanted to be left to die in peace.

George Washington died late on the Saturday night, less than 48 hours after being taken ill, a sufferer at the hands of heroic medicine and entirely a victim of it.

With hindsight, the question that strikes us now is how did the humoral theory and the reckless treatments of bleeding and purging go unchallenged for over 1600 years. The answer is that for all of that time medicine was a profession and not a science. The doctor went to a medical school and although what he learned there was almost all defective, he was credited with years of study and gained a standing in the community. He wore smart clothes of the conservative sort and a fine hat. Many were well meaning men.

The successful ones, aware that they had very few drugs that were at all effective, developed an impressive bedside manner. And to show that they were doing something for the patient, they purged and bled. They were professional men serving the community. Why should they go looking for cures beyond purging and bleeding?

There were of course doctors throughout history who made advances, physicians like Paracelsus and Sydenham. But their improvements were piecemeal. No doctor was a visionary on the scale of Newton, who saw a world of matter and motion and could not rest until he had provided explanations. Such a doctor would have thought: we are only playing at healing; our medicines do not work; we do not know what causes disease; we must find out.

Harvey discovered the circulation of the blood and published his *De Motu Cordis* in 1628, but he was not able to work out why blood was pumped around the body, nor how the blood got from arteries to the veins. Chemistry was in its infancy and oxygen was not discovered until 1772 by the Swiss apothecary Carl Wilhelm Scheele (Joseph Priestley did so independently in 1774 and got the credit) and the function of haemoglobin not until 1862, but arterial blood is so different from the darker venous blood that doctors had to be very uncurious not to seek the reason earlier. They avoided doing so by claiming that venous and arterial blood were two different substances. Venous blood was what you bled from a patient. Arterial blood you left well alone.

It was Malpighi, using an early microscope, who in 1661 examined lung tissue and saw how the arteries divided into capillaries in the alveoli, providing the missing link between arteries and veins. Malpighi was professor of medicine at Pisa. The man who took microscopy several stages further was a draper, Antoni van Leeuwenhoek. Leeuwenhoek was born in Delft, Holland, in 1632 and is thought to have had little scientific education. When his stepfather died in 1648 he was sent to Amsterdam as an apprentice to a linen draper. When he was 20 he returned to Delft and set himself up as a draper and haberdasher. His hobby was grinding lenses and his income was steady enough to allow him the time and money for this.

The compound microscopes of the time suffered from spherical and chromatic aberration and Leeuwenhoek overcame these defects by using tiny single lenses, in effect very small and extremely powerful magnifying glasses. Many were 2mm or less in diameter and Leeuwenhoek had the skill to grind them to a high magnification, some approaching 300 times. By 1674 he was examining bacteria and protozoa and later gave the first description of red blood cells, giving details of his work to the Royal Society in London, who elected him a fellow in 1680. These discoveries had huge significance but the medical profession ignored them and did not start taking an interest in microscopy until the 1830's. Doctors, like scientists, were happy to stay in their ignorance until evidence of their blindness stared them in the face.

The most striking example of medical intransigence in recent times concerns peptic ulcers. Because they were thought to be caused by stress, peptic ulcers were fashionable during the decades after World War II among top businessmen, as evidence that they were punishing themselves in the interests of their employers. Pepsin is a digestive enzyme secreted by the stomach lining along with hydrochloric acid, the acid-pepsin combination breaking down food proteins into peptones. Normally the gastric mucosa is chemically protected from attack by the acid-pepsin combination, but the defence mechanism can break down locally, especially in those individuals subjected to stress, and result in peptic ulceration. Gastric and duodenal ulcers are peptic ulcers found in the stomach and the duodenum respectively. That was the aetiology of peptic ulcers universally accepted by the medical profession until the early 1990's. Doctors could have changed their minds in the mid-1980's, but they would not listen.

The man that the medical profession would not listen to was a young Australian doctor, Barry Marshall. While doing his spell as trainee doctor in the pathological laboratory of a hospital on the edge of the Australian outback, Marshall was given the job of examining an archive of microscope slides of stomach tissue from patients who had been operated on. Marshall was struck by the presence in most of the tissue samples of specks with the twisted shape of a screw. They were the size of bacteria, but as every medical student knew, bacteria could not exist in the highly acidic environment of the stomach. A path lab colleague produced specimens of stomach tissue from patients currently in the hospital, and the bacteria-size specks were also invariably in evidence.

Marshall began to think the unthinkable, that a hitherto unknown bacterium could exist in stomach tissue. He even dared to think that it might be the cause of peptic ulceration. To prove that an organism was the cause of a disease, it was necessary to satisfy four criteria, known as Koch's postulates after the great pioneer bacteriologist who laid them down. Basically it meant that the organism must be discoverable in all instances of the disease, that the organism could be grown in pure culture and transferred to experimental animals and then recovered from the animals. Marshall set out to satisfy the Koch criteria and chose piglets as the experimental animals as pig physiology is in many respects nearest that of the human. His colleagues were surprised at the appearance in the path lab of a small piglet herd. The results with the piglets not being conclusive, Marshall, as with so many medical pioneers, decided that the only way of gaining proof was to experiment on himself. Marshall took a liquid broth culture of the bacteria he had harvested from stomach tissue and drank it down, saying afterwards that it tasted like sewer water.

After a week, Marshall began to vomit and feel ill, his breath was foul and endoscopy showed that his gastric mucosa was slimy and inflamed. If the textbooks and medical opinion had been right, nothing should have happened after drinking the culture fluid because bacteria cannot survive in the stomach. Marshall had proved them wrong. He named the new bacterium *Helicobacter pylori*, based on its twisted shape and its main site, the pylorus, the lower end of the stomach where it empties into the duodenum.

Persuading doctors was another matter. The world's distinguished gastroenterologists had spent their lives preaching that bacteria cannot survive in the stomach (although a few species with protective coats can pass through) and they were not going to admit they had been wrong. Especially not to a young Australian doctor with the ink on his qualifying certificate barely dry. In 1983, Marshall addressed a conference of the world's leading gastroenterologists and he received about as much support as Galileo did when he appeared before the Roman Catholic hierarchy.

But Marshall did not retract. He returned to his hospital and worked on treatments to eliminate *Helicobacter*. Although peptic ulcers are rarely life-threatening, gastric ulcers that are not healed can turn cancerous. Marshall started off using bismuth compounds since there was a long history of these giving relief to ulcer patients. It was found that the common antibiotic amoxicillin was also successful, especially when combined with metronidazole. In the final treatment that gave the best results, a third ingredient, a proton pump inhibitor was included. This kept down stomach acid and allowed ulcers to heal.

Eventually the evidence for *Helicobacter* and its role in peptic ulceration became so overwhelming that even the medical profession was obliged to submit. Barry Marshall was given a prestigious appointment with the United University of Virginia, in the United States, going from outcast to guru almost overnight.

The period of Galenic medicine, from about 200 A.D. to the middle of the 19th Century, was one of the few periods in history, at least in the field of medicine, where the poor came off better than those who had money. Not being able to afford doctors' fees, the poor made do with herbal remedies from the local wise women, those that is who survived being burned as witches. It was acceptable for men, as authenticated professionals, to purge and bleed their patients excruciatingly, but if the local healing woman became too proficient with her herbs and natural remedies, and effected cures harmlessly, she was a candidate for a ride in the ducking stool or for cindering at the stake.

There are scores of accounts of how royalty and notables were purged and bled insufferably and, it seems clear to us now, to death. Philip II of Spain suffered perhaps worst of any, in 1598 undergoing a prolonged purging and bleeding assault by his physicians and lying in his own filth because he was in too much pain to be moved. The tooth-grinding account in Carlos Eire's *From Madrid to Purgatory* details how the torture went on for two months. The poor could not afford the luxury of medical intervention on such a scale.

Fortunately for the rest of the world, Galen's stranglehold on medicine was confined to Europe. In India, ayurvedic medicine developed gradually from earlier forms and although some false doctrines evolved – three bodily humours were postulated: wind, bile and phlegm – the approach was altogether more holistic than in Western medicine and heroic blood-letting and purging were unknown. In China, medicine was advanced from early times by the concept of a healing force called *Chi*. The Romanised spelling, rather perversely, is *Qi*, that word so useful in Scrabble for getting rid of the Q late in the game, but we will keep things simple and stick to Chi. It is so obvious that there is a force at work in the body that wants to keep it well and, when it is sick, to make it better, that it is surprising that only the Chinese recognized this. By not doing so, Western medicine lost a great opportunity. .

Although Western medicine has ignored Chi, the healing force – there is not even a name for it – doctors in the West have been forced to take notice of one of its manifestations, acupuncture. While doctors in Europe were purging and bleeding their patients to the point of death, the Chinese were demonstrating that many illnesses could be cured by inserting needles into key points in the skin, a procedure which harnessed the body's healing force. Such however has been the arrogance of the medical profession in the West that when acupuncture spread into Europe and America after the Second World War, it was regarded as another quaint oriental departure from 'true' medicine, the Western sort that had held on to humoral theory and violent purging and bleeding until the middle of the 19th Century.

In 2007 a film was shown on television of Chinese open heart surgery, attended by Western surgeons, carried out with acupuncture as the sole anaesthetic. The patient was conscious and able to talk with the surgeons carrying out the operation. The huge advantages of carrying out surgery with a conscious and cooperative patient are of course at present only available to the Chinese because only they have the belief that has come from centuries of successful experience of acupuncture. For the same reason acupuncture is the first choice of most mainland Chinese women for anaesthesia in childbirth.

To understand why Western medicine has failed to take advantage of acupuncture and other techniques that harness the body's healing force, we have to examine Western medical thinking. In particular we have to take a look at the placebo effect.

Credit for the discovery of the placebo effect, the alleviation of medical symptoms by non-therapeutic agencies, is usually given to Henry Beecher. Beecher discovered the potency of placebos in the setting where many medical breakthroughs were made, on the battlefield. Beecher was an anaesthetist in the United States army and, during the closing stages of the Second World War, his medical unit frequently ran out of morphine injections. On one occasion, faced with treating a soldier with horrific injuries and without morphine to relieve the pain, Beecher was surprised when a nurse injected the patient with saline solution. He was even more surprised when the injured soldier responded as if he had been given morphine and went through the subsequent operation with only mild discomfort. To Beecher's amazement, the patient also failed to exhibit the usual post-operative surgical shock.

Beecher was somewhat naive, since for decades it had been the practice of night sisters on hospital wards to give restless patients injections an injection of sterile saline solution to ensure them a good night's sleep. But his curiosity had been aroused and he was so impressed by this wartime experience that after the war he assembled a team at Harvard to study the effects of suggestion or, as it became known, the 'placebo effect'. The outcome was the publication of Beecher's paper 'The Powerful Placebo' in the *Journal of the American Medical Association* in 1955. Beecher's paper has been rightly criticised for failing to compare his groups of patients receiving placebos with groups receiving no treatment, meaning that the improvements he attributed to placebos could have been due to spontaneous remission of symptoms or to the normal fluctuations in their severity. The irony is that Beecher went on to pioneer the placebo-controlled clinical trial of new drugs, rightly arguing that any observed improvement must be compared with the improvements produced by a placebo. A later development of the placebo-controlled trial, the double-blind trial where neither prescriber nor patient knows whether the drug or the placebo is being administered, has now become the gold standard for the clinical trials of new drugs or the comparison of established ones.

By the time Western medicine had discovered Chi, the body's healing force, the medical profession's faith had been firmly placed in the new drugs pouring from the pharmaceutical laboratories, and this great natural boon became labelled as the placebo effect, a nuisance that interfered with clinical trials. Ignoring the body's natural healing power led to medicine taking itself too seriously. Drugs were all, patients becoming simply the passive recipients of pharmaceuticals.

Even surgery became blind to the contribution made by the body's natural healing forces. This was illustrated when a perceptive American surgeon became intrigued by the fact that all his patients on whom he performed knee arthroscopies reported an improvement. Arthroscopy involves penetrating a joint, usually the knee, and examining its condition by means of a small lens. The surgeon cannot make significant repairs using this procedure, but is able to wash out the joint and smooth rough areas. The surgeon decided to compare five patients who had the normal procedure with five who were simply given dummy incisions in their knees to convince them they had undergone the actual operation. All ten patients were followed up and after two years the patients who had had the sham surgery claimed as much pain relief as those who had undergone the actual procedure.

Following the announcement that implanting embryo stem cells into the brains of Alzheimer patients produced benefits, two American surgeons decided to test whether placebo effects contributed to any of the reported improvements. In one study, Professor Thomas Freeman, of the University of South Florida, compared 12 patients who had received stem cell implants with the same number who had a dummy capsule inserted, citing as justification the dangerousness of the implant operation. Not only was there no danger in the dummy procedure, but some recipients showed the same degree of mental improvement as those who had stem cells implanted. In both medicine and surgery, it is clear that many physicians and surgeons are undervaluing the contribution made by the body's natural healing force, although this need not prevent individuals from tapping into its power by the exercise of positive thinking.

Few doctors after Hippocrates were as honest about the limitations of medicine as the founder had been, although one famously was. Oliver Wendell Holmes, a qualified lawyer and a humorist as well as being professor of anatomy at Harvard from 1847 – 82, was refreshingly blunt about the deficiencies of medicine in his time: '.............. and I firmly believe that if the whole material medica, as now used, could be sunk to the bottom of the sea, it would be all the better for mankind – and all the worse for the fishes.'

By the late 1950's when, following the publicity resulting from Beecher's paper on the placebo effect, Western medicine was absorbing the idea that therapeutic effects could be obtained by non-therapeutic substances or procedures, the first medicaments of the great drug bonanza of the second half of the 20th century were beginning to pour from the pharmaceutical companies. Penicillin had been followed by streptomycin, chloramphenicol and the tetracycline antibiotics. Chlorpromazine, the first of the mood modifying drugs, had been launched, and the first fully effective drugs against blood pressure were imminent. Excitement about the seemingly endless possibilities for new drugs obscured investigation of the harnessing of the placebo effect for use as a tool in conventional medicine. That sort of thing could be left to the Chinese.

But the Chinese and Indians were not entirely alone in discovering unorthodox therapies. A German, Samuel Hahnemann, born in 1755 and qualifying as a physician in 1799, trod the medical path of the day, bleeding and purging, until he was sickened by its barbarity. He then gave up the orthodox approach and began looking at traditional herbal treatments. When translating the materia medica of a Dr Cullen, a Scot, Hahnemann took exception to Cullen's attribution of the efficacy of cinchona in the treatment of malaria to its tonic action on the stomach.

Cinchona was effective because it contained quinine, but Hahnemann came up with another theory. Having dosed himself with cinchona for several days and claiming to have developed all the symptoms of malarial intermittent fever, he concluded that cinchona was effective because it produced the same symptoms as the disease. Hahnemann was not the first to propose the medical theory that like cures like – it was a common belief in German folk medicine – but he pioneered using the theory as the basis for a whole new branch of healing.

When Hahnemann became a professor at the Leipzig University school of medicine, he set up a series of 'provings', experiments with a chosen band of students to determine the physical, emotional and mental reactions of healthy individuals to various plants and minerals. He then proposed that diseases should be treated by small doses of those substances that produced the symptoms of that disease in healthy persons. He called the system homeopathy.

Hahnemann was lucky with his timing. Bleeding and purging were at their height and there was no attempt in orthodox medicine to harness the Chi, the body's natural healing force. Many of the public and a few doctors - although most were virulently against homeopathy - took to the idea of an alternative treatment to heroic assaults on the bodies of ill people. There is no need to dwell on the unscientific nature of homeopathy and its unproven claim that the more diluted the solution of a medicament the more potent is its action. If nothing else, homeopathy stimulates the Chi and does so naturally, without side effects, and for minor conditions is a sensible choice. The more obsessive homeopaths claim all sorts of cures for homeopathy in more serious conditions, but they, like the other practitioners of alternative therapies, head for a doctor's surgery and a prescription for antibiotics when they get a potentially dangerous infection.

During the last few decades, there has been a proliferation in the number of alternative therapies offered and in those availing themselves of such treatments. The more rigid supporters of orthodox medicine bewail this tendency as another sign of New Age sorcery, without seeming to grasp that it is the frontal assault approach of orthodox medicine that has driven people to seek less intrusive and more holistic therapies. Conventional medicines are too often sledgehammers to crack nuts.

Paul Ehrlich, one of the great pioneers of early research into the potential of synthetic chemicals for use as medicines, studied the body's antibody response to bacterial invasion in the 1880's and marvelled at the way antibodies targeted the invaders so specifically. He called them magic bullets and spent his working life looking for drugs that possessed the same specificity. Ehrlich and his team turned their attention to finding a cure for syphilis and screened over 600 organic arsenic compounds for activity against the causative organism, *Treponema pallidum*, then known as *Spirochaeta pallida*. Compound number 606, marketed as *Salvarsan*, proved effective and revolutionised the treatment of syphilis, but it was far from a magic bullet.

Like all arsenical compounds, *Salvarsan* at effective dosage was bordering on toxic levels and produced severe side effects. It had the additional disadvantage of needing to be given by intravenous injection (Alexander Fleming was one of the few doctors in London licensed to administer the drug, which provided a useful additional income in the days when he was lowly paid and unknown). To prevent the drug's oxidation the ampoules had to be filled with an inert gas and, once injected, a rapid and potentially fatal anaphylactic reaction could occur, which required the immediate injection of adrenaline.

Ehrlich's original models for his magic bullets had been human antitoxins, and the reason they were so effective and free from undesirable reactions was that they were produced by the body. Synthetic chemicals produced in a laboratory proved to be a very different matter, blunderbusses rather than rifles. The sledgehammer/blunderbuss effect, with the body being subjected to off-the-target side effects, is the price we have to pay for having a pill for every ill and it is not surprising that frequently the side effects of the cure can seem worse than the illness.

Having entered pharmacy at the time when penicillin first became available for general prescribing and witnessed the subsequent continuous flow of new drugs in the second half of the 20th Century, I was an unquestioning supporter of synthetic drugs. As the first pharmacist to live and work in Borneo, I had helped to bring their benefits to people who had not yet seen a radio or a motor car. The first crack in my belief in modern medicine occurred many years later when I owned my own pharmacy. Mr Spark came into the pharmacy perhaps half a dozen times a year wearing a broad grin and buzzing with energy. He had fingers in a number of pies but without fail he would come in at the beginning of December extolling the virtues of this year's Christmas trees, and I always bought one.

One autumn Mr Spark got bronchitis and went to the village doctor for the first time for twenty years. The infection cleared up with a course of antibiotics, but the doctor discovered that Mr Spark's blood pressure was well above average and prescribed heavyweight antihypertensives and told him to come back in two weeks. When Mr Spark's repeat prescription came into the dispensary in a fortnight, I asked my senior assistant who had brought the prescription in. When she said that it was Mr Spark, for a moment I disbelieved her. The shop was in silence, with none of the hearty bantering we were used to. I went out with the prescription to find a hunched pale faced character leaning against the counter. He had a hangdog look and in a quavering voice said, 'The doctor's very pleased with me'. I muttered some platitude and retired to the dispensary to contemplate a man cut down in his prime by medication.

It was the first dent in my belief in the new age of therapeutics. Mr Spark's doctor had simply been obeying the NHS guidelines. Those with blood pressure higher than the 90 mm diastolic limit were required to be put on antihypertensive drugs. Extensive trials had shown that this gave a proportion of treated individuals patients two to four years of extra life compared with those who went untreated. The guidelines were explicit. Blood pressure higher than the norm was to be reduced. No allowance was made for the Mr Sparks, whose energy and enthusiasm was fuelled by higher than average blood pressure, nor for the fact that blood pressure goes up naturally with age, due to hardening of the arteries, to compensate for the slowing down of the metabolic rate. So focused had Mr Spark's doctor been on the readings on the sphygmomanometer, and so gratified that the levels were now within the laid down government guidelines, that he had overlooked the deterioration in his patient's condition.

At about that time I went for a blood pressure check and as my own diastolic blood pressure was over 90mm my doctor wanted to put me on medication. I told him about Mr Spark, without mentioning him by name, and declined treatment. Five years or so later I took a course of transcendental meditation and, monitoring my own blood pressure, I noticed that it had gone down. Fifteen years later, my reading is 130/80.

Doctors need guidelines, but they should be seen as guides and not cast iron moulds into which everyone must fit regardless of age, size, shape and personality. The Mr Sparks of this world should be given the choice between remaining dynamic or becoming a healthier vegetable with the possibility of a few extra years of vegetating.

The mystery of the last sixty years of the National Health Service is that we live longer but need more medical attention than in pre-NHS days. One of the reasons is that people are living longer. The other is that health has become a preoccupation.

The Beveridge report of 1945, which first outlined the concept of a free health service, included estimates of the cost of the various branches of the welfare state. In 1945 the annual cost of state pensions was £126m and was forecast to rise to £300m after twenty years. Health expenditure by the state, on the other hand, costing £170m annually when the NHS was set up, was forecast to be still at that level twenty years later. This was on the basis that after an initial period of increased expenditure to tackle poverty-related diseases and to promote health education, the nation's health would improve. It was believed that, in spite of a growing population, health costs would be reduced per capita because people would be healthier.

What the founders of the NHS were unable to visualise was a nation that was healthier but more preoccupied with health. Health, with the full concurrence of the government and most of the population, has become a major subject for the media. We are encouraged by the government health mandarins, aided and abetted by the newspapers and television, to be concerned about our weight and diet, whether we should eat proteins and carbohydrates in the same meal, or fat at all. We are prompted to worry whether the filmwrap around our sandwiches, or decaffeinated coffee, is going to give us cancer, if there is salmonella or listeria in supermarket chicken and eggs, whether signals from the nearby electricity pylon or telephone mast are vitiating our brains. Every newspaper must contain articles about health or threats to it. Whole magazines are devoted to improving our fitness and safeguarding our health, as if *Homo sapiens* were a fragile endangered species whose survival could only be assured by intensive concentration on health minutiae.

This is a recent development. Until the mid-19th century, when there were very few effective drugs, individuals had to be more stoical about illness, and about death. Children going down with diphtheria or scarlet fever, or an adult contracting pneumonia, would be lucky if they survived. Now that we do not need to concern ourselves with such hazards, we worry more. We have become health neurotics. We need to take care of our environment, but we need not mollycoddle our bodies.

It would be bad enough if health neuroticism were confined to the general public, but it is has infected the experts. Given that most of these are men it should not be surprising that the obsession with health has been taken to extremes because that is what males in authority do, even though the health supremos are supposed to be scientists. We have only to look at the great salt controversy to see how readily senior medical officers are prepared to promote health scares on the basis of a theories not backed by real evidence.

The condemnation of salt is generally reckoned to have started in 1978 with the publication of a paper by Lillian Gleibermann, an anthropologist at Michigan University, reviewing 27 studies in which the urine of indigenous tribes on low salt intake, who suffer few heart attacks or strokes, was compared with that of high salt intake individuals in industrialized societies prone to strokes and coronary attacks. The inference was that excessive salt intake caused these episodes. In fact, suspicions about salt had arisen much earlier. At a dinner party I gave in Sarawak in 1959, a WHO doctor friend, who later became a high executive in the WHO hierarchy in Geneva, announced that salt was responsible for high blood pressure, and therefore strokes and coronary attacks. His pronouncement caused an argument so intemperate that it spoiled the dinner. Sometimes, it seems, in medicine as in other fields, an idea forms, circulates, and waits for a catalyst to bring it into prominence, regardless of its veracity.

In the United Kingdom the main protagonist of the dangers of salt is Graham MacGregor, professor of cardiovascular medicine at St George's Medical School, London, whose view is that salt causes water retention, the excess fluid causing a strain on the heart leading to high blood pressure and, as a result, 120,000 preventable deaths a year in Britain alone. The WHO came to take much the same view and there came general acceptance of the dangers of a high salt intake throughout the medical profession in most of the world. In 2004 , the Food Standards Agency in Britain ran a £4million Sid the Slug advertising campaign publicising the dangers of salt and recommending an intake of six grams or less a day. At a time when the authorities were trying to get school children to eat more vegetables with their dinners, salt was removed from school dinner tables, making carrots and greens even less appealing than before.

It is not necessary to detail here the catalogue of conflicting medical articles over the years, some supporting the salt scare and others rebutting it, since in the *British Medical Journal* in 2002 reviewed all the major salt studies and concluded that a low-salt diet does reduce blood pressure, but to a minuscule extent, 1mm of mercury, an amount not detectable on the blood pressure machines in doctors' surgeries. Despite this, most of the medical profession and a whole section of the general public continue to behave as if salt were a danger to the nation's health. Butter and milk have suffered the same sort of smear campaign as salt, and are equally innocent victims of the paranoia of the male health pundits.

To get a balanced perspective on health, it is useful to look at the Caucasians. Soon after the end of the Second World War a U.K. medical team went out to the Caucasus mountains to study communities whose members were thought to live to great ages. Many individuals were believed to live until they were 115 or 120. The team carried out thorough physical examinations and took full life histories and, from the events remembered by older individuals, were able to confirm that some were undoubtedly living a decade or more beyond their centenaries. What surprised the doctors, however, were the heart X-rays of these mountain dwellers. Most showed the marked heart muscle scarring characteristic of severe coronary attacks. When those showing the cardiac scarring were questioned about an earlier serious illness, all denied any recollection of such an event. Some, when pressed, could just remember being off colour for a few days and resting in bed.

The Caucasians studied lived on a simple healthy diet and most walked long distances herding or visiting far-flung communities with loads on their backs. All lived above 6000 feet (2460 metres). These factors undoubtedly contributed to their health and longevity. What no doubt contributed as much was their complete acceptance of good health. They had no conception of heart attacks and thus no fear of them, or of any other illness.

We cannot go back to living in the innocent Eden of the Caucasians. We can however remember their example and skip the health pages in the newspaper, forget about the latest diet craze, ignore our bodies and assume they will be adequate for our needs. Most of us need meditation and stillness to accept such an assured state, and we need to set aside time for their practice.

Some months ago, when I was in the middle of writing this book, I developed an intermittent but severe pain in the bone at the top of my left foot which the podiatrist could not diagnose or suggest any treatment for, other than analgesics. The book to which I owe the credit for any progress I have made along the spiritual path, *A Course In Miracles*, teaches that we only retain a sickness if it serves a purpose. Any illness can be cured by our deciding that it no longer has a use. I have had great difficulty in accepting this concept and little opportunity to try it out since I am mostly well. However, some years ago I developed indigestion and was found to have a *Helicobacter* infection. This was treated, but I was left with occasional indigestion which my doctor put down to a sensitive gastric mucosa following the infection, and he prescribed a proton pump inhibitor (ppi) to be taken each morning. This lowered the stomach acid level and kept me free of symptoms.

Aware of the *Miracles* teaching, I occasionally thought I ought to dispense with the problem and the treatment, but lack of belief prevented me. When I had my foot problem, I came home from the podiatrist, sat down and decided that the foot pain served no purpose. I would dispense with it. The pain went – and in fact never came back – and the next morning I was on the point of taking my ppi tablet when I realized the absurdity of the situation. I had got rid of the foot pain, yet I was prepared to hang on to my stomach problem. I made the decision there and then to dispense with the indigestion, put the tablets away and have not needed to take them since.

Renouncing prescribed drugs is not a course to be taken lightly and only after discussion with one's doctor, but there is no doubt that a substantial proportion of the medication going down the nation's throats is unnecessary and a consequence of the lingering convention that when a patient complains the doctor must prescribe. Part of the enlightenment of the New Dawn will be a growing awareness that we are provided free of charge with the most effective health safeguard, Chi, nature's healing force.

25

THE NEW DAWN HERE AND NOW

have lived in Yorkshire for most of my adult life, a county where now most are materially well-off but where that was not always so. Folk wisdom arises in hard times and it was the poorest who looked at their supposed betters and came up with that wisest of Yorkshire sayings: 'Much wants more'. Which sums up the dissatisfaction of many people in the present world. Inherent in those three words of Yorkshire wisdom is the truth that the craving for more is a sign of inner discontent.

Most governments, most businessmen and most economists, the men who have run things until now, have pinned their hopes on the free market as the universal panacea. Until the beginning of this year their hopes appeared to have been fulfilled. The economies of industrialized nations were thriving, with inflation kept low by cheap imports from China and the developing world. House prices would continue to rise, the experts said, because demand would continue to exceed the supply. Builders rushed to put up more houses and the banks, the guardians of the country's wealth, lent extravagantly.

We have now been brought to our senses. We do not yet know the full consequences of the present debt crisis, whether it will be an old-type recession or something worse. What I have known, ever since being given the revelation of the New Dawn, is that the wider spiritual awakening would not arrive until the debt-fuelled cloud-cuckoo-land economic boom had burst. There will be much agonizing during the difficult times ahead, but for those with eyes to see, the halt in the mad spree of free-for-all consumerism will be viewed as a sign of hope. The world needed a shock to jolt it into reality. Disillusion with materialism is the prerequisite for the spiritual awakening that has already begun. The New Dawn signals the arrival of a time of hope.

Those used to a life of unquestioning materialism will ask how life can be run on love. The question that needs to be asked is how can any sort of meaningful life be run on a treadmill to accumulate material goods. Love is not an airy fairy refuge for those who do not wish to compete. Applying love to all aspects of life is full-time and demanding, but it rewards the giver and receiver of love with the unsurpassed gifts of peace and joy.

Love is clear on the issue of crime. It is not just to criminals, nor loving, to let them continue in their mistaken ways. By allowing criminals to carry on their activities, as we are doing in many parts of the country, we are declaring that we do not care about them or their victims. The only loving policy towards crime is zero tolerance. Criminals of whatever kind must be restrained and then shown a better way.

The same applies to terrorists. It is not right or just, nor is it productive, to confine without trial in torture camps those suspected of terrorism. Torture confirms what the terrorist believes, that his opponents are inhuman. Terrorists, as with criminals, need to be treated as fellow human beings and to be shown that love is a better way than hatred. Love is stronger than any other human attribute, the most powerful force at our disposal, and translated into practical form, love is the solution to terrorism, as it is the solution to every other human dilemma.

When going through the text of this book, checking spelling and correcting grammatical slips, I had an unnerving experience. I found myself reading the text through the eyes of a sceptic, with almost every sentence seeming improbable and unbelievable. I was flattened by the thought that I had wasted fifteen months on a book that would not be taken seriously. While in this despondent state, I read an article in the newspaper about an Irish woman, Lorna Byrne, whose first memories as an infant were of seeing and communing with angels, an experience that has stayed with her throughout her life and which she has described in a book, *Angels In My Hair*. I read the book and my despair melted away.

Lorna Byrne had a torrid time at school. Being preoccupied with her angels, she was diagnosed as retarded, but she had help from an angel dressed in a cape, who looked like a professor. I had pondered long and hard as to whom the Lecturer might be, and I had been aware of a gentler guide during the later stages of the book. It now seemed clear that they were my angel collaborators, and that one of the great discoveries of the New Dawn will be people's growing awareness of their celestial helpers.

We are on the verge of a time of hope and there are increasing signs of the breaking of the New Dawn. In Turkey, the mullahs are going through a revision of the Muslim traditions, the *hadith*, aimed at lessening the restrictions on women imposed by harsher Islamic male interpreters. This may appear a small step, but it is a hugely significant one.

Those waiting for the day when Muslim women will have a say in their religion, will be heartened by developments in Morocco. King Mohammed VI is an enlightened ruler and one of the liberal reforms he has instigated is the training of women to become *mourchidat*, Islamic female priests (the word literally translates as 'female guide').

On succeeding the throne after the death of his harshly repressive father, King Hassan II, King Mohammed VI promised openness and democracy, and announced his championship of women's rights by abolishing the royal harem of 40 women. In 2003, he took the unprecedented step of inviting a woman, el Mekkaoui, to give the Ramadan lecture at the royal palace in Rabat attended by senior members of the government and the armed forces and foreign ambassadors. This elevation of a woman in front of imams from all over the Islamic world helped pave the way for the *mourchidat* movement, enabling women to go to their local *mourchidat* for advice and support. What is significant about the women's movement in Morocco is that women feel that they are being liberated through the original teachings of the Prophet, not through imitating the women's lib model of the West.

The Christian Church nowadays hits the news with crisis headlines. The Pope is obliged to visit countries to apologise for the sexual abuse inflicted by Catholic priests, and the Anglican Church is split by the imagined twin assaults of homosexuality and women bishops. And yet, among the holy ruins, there stands a man who exuberantly lives out the love and joy that Jesus came to proclaim. It need not surprise us that the man, who is black, is Dr John Sentamu, the Archbishop of York, because such marvels will be a feature of the New Dawn.

Since its foundation, America has been the bastion of world democracy. The American people have from the outset given hope and a home to those coming from countries going through times when hope, and often freedom, did not exist. Democracies, by their nature, have their ups and downs and the United States has been through a period of illusion, imagining that the imposition of financial and military muscle is what counts in the world. America has overstretched itself financially, for the worst of reasons, through overstretching itself militarily.

America is coming back to realizing that what matters is freedom of the human spirit. The New Dawn will herald many scarcely believable happenings, one of which will occur in November 2008 when getting on for half of the population of the United States will vote for a party with a woman Vice-President or, within a decade of 9/11, for a black President whose middle name is Hussein. The American people are ready to experience inspiration and hope again.

From an aeroplane at night you can still see the world's cities ablaze with light. With the planet short of energy it would make sense to turn them off, but the dazzle uplifts us and we are reluctant to face the dark. It has not sunk in yet that we do not need the blaze of city lights to confirm that we are alive and functioning. Deep in each one of us there is all the assurance and light we need. We simply need to pause, to go inside ourselves, and to listen.

The New Dawn is not an organisation. It is not a movement you join. The New Dawn is a message of hope in the minds of people who seek personal freedom. Each one of us is a God-created being with the ability to realise our potential, and the purpose of this life is to use the power of love to fully express our creativity. It does not matter that our ideas about a heavenly entity are uncertain and hesitant. The experience is real.

BOOK SUGGESTIONS

LIFE-CHANGING

A Course In Miracles 3rd Edition, Foundation for Inner Peace ISBN 978-1-883360-24-5

Journey Beyond Words Brent Haskell, DeVorss Publications   ISBN 087516-695-4

INSPIRATIONAL

No Destination: An Autobiography Satish Kumar,   Dartington Resurgence
                                                    ISBN 1870098897

Angels In My Hair Lorna Byrne, Century   ISBN 9781846051777

Rachel Carson Linda Lear, Allen Lane   ISBN 0-713-99236-0

The Transformed Mind: Reflections On Truth, Love And Happiness
His Holiness The Dalai Lama, Hodder & Stoughton   ISBN 0-340-76948-3

Dreams From My Father Barack Obama, Canongate   ISBN 9781847670946

George Müller: Delighted In God Roger Steer, Christian Focus ISBN1-85792-340-5

INFORMATIVE

1421: The Year That China Discovered The World Gavin Menzies, Bantam
                                                    ISBN 0593050789

Demonic Males: Apes And The Origins Of Human Violence Richard Wrangham &
Dale Peterson, Bloomsbury   ISBN 0-7475-3142-0

The Structure of Scientific Revolutions Thomas Kuhn, University of Chicago Press
                                                    ISBN 0-226-45804-0

Silent Spring Rachel Carson, Penguin   ISBN 9780141184944

The God Delusion Richard Dawkins, Bantam   ISBN 9780593055489

Argonauts Of The Western Pacific Bronislaw Malinowski, Routledge   1922
 No 65 in the series of Monographs by writers connected with the London School of
Economics and Political Science